New Thinking on Leadership

New Thinking on Leadership

A global perspective

Edited by Hilarie Owen

KoganPage

LONDON PHILADELPHIA NEW DELHI

First published in Great Britain and the United States in 2012 by Kogan Page Limited

120 Pentonville Road
London N1 9JN
United Kingdom
www.koganpage.com

1518 Walnut Street, Suite 1100
Philadelphia PA 19102
USA

4737/23 Ansari Road
Daryaganj
New Delhi 110002
India

ISBN   978 0 7494 6633 6
E-ISBN   978 0 7494 6634 3

British Library Cataloguing-in-Publication Data

A CIP record for this book is available from the British Library.

Library of Congress Cataloging-in-Publication Data

New thinking on leadership : a global perspective / [edited by] Hilarie Owen.
    p. cm.
    ISBN 978-0-7494-6633-6 – ISBN 978-0-7494-6634-3   1. Leadership.   I. Owen, Hilarie.
    BF637.L4N49 2012
    303.3'4–dc23

                                                                    2012020104

Typeset by Graphicraft Limited, Hong Kong
Printed and bound in India by Replika Press Pvt Ltd

CONTENTS

NOTES ON CONTRIBUTORS

Elena P Antonacopoulou is a Professor of Organizational Behaviour at University of Liverpool Management School, where she leads GNOSIS – a global research initiative advancing actionable knowledge. She is widely published in leading international journals on themes such as change, learning, knowledge and leadership practices in organizations, and on the development of new methodologies for studying social complexity.

Warren Bennis is University Professor and Distinguished Professor of Business Administration at the University of Southern California and author of *Still Surprised: A memoir of a life in leadership*.

Keith Grint is Professor of Public Leadership at Warwick University. He has held chairs at Cranfield and Lancaster Universities and is a founding co-editor of the journal *Leadership* (Sage). His books include *The Arts of Leadership* (2000), *Leadership: Limits and possibilities* (2005) and *Leadership: A very short introduction* (2010).

Dr Jesus A Sampedro Hidalgo holds a doctorate in strategic leadership (DSL) and an MBA from Regent University (Virginia, USA). He is also an LLC certified leadership coach. His books include *A Leadership Framework for Transformation*, he has published many articles and is editor of a leadership blog (**www.recursosparalideres.blogspot.com**). He is founder of Global Leadership Consulting, a leadership training and consulting firm (**www.glcconsulting.com.ve**).

Fiona Kennedy works as a senior leadership facilitator and researcher at the New Zealand Leadership Institute. She has recently published a chapter on constructionist approaches to leadership development with her colleagues at the Institute (F Kennedy, B Carroll, J Francoeur and B Jackson (in press), A tale of two perspectives: an account of entity and social constructionist approaches to 'conflict' in leadership development, in *Advancing Leadership Theory: A conversation among perspectives*, edited by Mary Uhl Bien and Sonia Osprina).

Jiacheng Li is Associate Professor in the School of Education Science at the East China Normal University, Shanghai, China. Focusing on school leadership, he is the author of *Caring for Life: School reform in China* (2006), and co-author of *School Leadership Reform in China* (2007) and *School Life and Student Development* (2009).

Tracey T Manning, PhD, is a US-based leadership development consultant and part-time faculty member at the University of Maryland College Park, teaching graduate leadership courses for the Health Services Administration Department. An applied social psychologist with over 30 years of experience, she researched early childhood influences on leadership effectiveness, and coordinates a Legacy Leadership Institute for the Environment to train high-level environmental volunteers.

Hilarie Owen was originally a political scientist and had a corporate career before writing several books on leadership that have sold globally. She was Head of Leadership Services for the Police in England, Wales and Northern Ireland, and today runs the UK-based Institute of Leadership, working around the world.

Brian Patterson is coach to senior executives and leadership teams with Praesta Ireland. He was previously CEO of Waterford Wedgwood, and Chairman of *The Irish Times* and of Vodafone Ireland. He is Chairman of two emerging companies – ORRECO and scurri.com – and lectures on leadership at the Irish Management Institute.

Sangeeth Varghese is a globally acknowledged leadership thinker, ranked among the top 10 by the Bombay Stock Exchange, and the founder of LeadCap, one of the world's biggest youth leadership movements. He is the author of the 2011 No 1 business bestseller in India, *Open Source Leader*, and the South Asia bestseller *Decide to Lead*. He was nominated as a Young Global Leader in 2010 by the World Economic Forum, Davos. He was educated at the Harvard Kennedy School and the London School of Economics.

PREFACE

Leadership has become such a common concept these days that it is now treated with scepticism. People accept that leadership is needed but they are also deeply mistrustful about our so-called leaders in society. Yet around the world it is clear that there is still a hunger to understand this concept and to value it. It is leadership that is required rather than leaders. But is this possible?

I have been fortunate to work with some amazing people and my request for some of them to contribute to this book was greeted positively. I asked if they could write about their passion on leadership rather than a collection of academic papers. What were their thoughts and questions and ideas?

While there was a plan for the book, it soon became clear that the plan had to go. As an experienced author I was comfortable with the ebb and flow of writing books, so I decided to just see what occurred. The book is an unfolding story of how a concept around the world is changing. While academics say 'the leader as hero is gone,' here is how leadership is actually changing on a global scale, with examples from different countries.

I wish to thank all those who have contributed and have shown their own courage and leadership in writing what is something quite unique and different. I also thank the team involved from Kogan Page. It has been a real pleasure to edit and contribute to this book.

Leadership is still needed in the world and it is hoped this book will inspire individuals not only to read and learn but act to transform their own organizations so that leadership can be unleashed.

Hilarie Owen

Introduction
Leadership crisis – what leadership crisis?

HILARIE OWEN

For over 30 years now leadership has dominated programmes, books and training departments. At the beginning of the 21st Century an internet search on leadership resulted in around 10,000 findings; 12 years later, in 2012, a search on leadership produced around 400,000 items. In the UK the public sector in particular has been focusing on leadership, which is interesting because prior to the government setting up the Centre for Excellence and Management in London, there were meetings undertaken by civil servants from the Department of Education. Those invited included the Chair of the British Chamber of Commerce, Chris Humphreys, John Adair, myself and others. At this stage the idea was to bring all of us together to address the issue of a 'management crisis' in the UK. It was a very controlled meeting and over lunch I spoke to one of the civil servants and remarked: 'You are leaving out an even more important issue: leadership.' To which she replied: 'We don't want to touch leadership; it's too much of a hot potato!'

Well the 'hot potato' has come back to burn them. The public sector went on to set up the Leadership Council in the NHS, the National College of School Leadership and the Centre for Strategic Leadership for civil servants themselves. The cost of these has been huge. Has leadership improved as a result? The question this raises is: Can you teach leadership?

In the private sector, there has been reluctance by executives to develop their leadership once in a senior role. The Work Foundation found (2009) that board directors and chief executives are far less likely to receive any leadership development than their junior managers. There seems to be an attitude of: 'We are at the top, we don't have anything else to learn.' Or is it that they see leadership development as something they won't benefit from because those who deliver it know less than themselves?

For over three decades, organizations across the UK in the public and private sectors have spent millions trying to develop leadership. Why? It is widely recognized that effective leadership is fundamental, especially when change or transformation is required. The topic is certainly regarded as a priority for organizations. Yet most leadership training or courses fail to have lasting effects on the leadership behaviour of their participants. How can leadership development initiatives unlock leadership potential and build leadership effectiveness? One thing is certain: if organizations keep conducting the same programmes, or sending their managers/professionals to the same programmes, research indicates they will see the same minimal results.

The reality is, we seem to be seeing less leadership in the world and it is being replaced with corruption and misbehaviour by our so-called leaders. From bankers, sports bodies, corporate directors and politicians, the world seems to be going in the opposite direction from moral, transforming, authentic leadership. It is a fact that those with positional authority to lead have failed us. Or are there other factors, maybe even factors we don't want to explore, at play?

The philosopher Nietzsche believed that each one of us is alone, living in an uncaring world, where the strong become stronger and the weak are inferior and will perish. Those who lead are the strong willed who were born to lead and the rest are a burden. It was interesting that in the recent Budget Statement from the Chancellor in the House of Commons, he called the elderly 'a burden'. Are we seeing this underlying philosophy behind what has been happening in the last few years? Does this explain why so many of those in positions of authority had the belief that taking more expenses than they were entitled to was their right? Or why they saw nothing wrong in running a company or bank into the ground, or risking people's savings?

In the last 50 years Western society has focused more on personality than character, with the latter having moral standards and values. It has been the age of the personality and short-term gains. Community and caring have been replaced with self-fulfilment and gratification. Collectively, government after government have led us to where we are today for they have implemented – and still are implementing – the policies that resulted in this.

In business, the drive for shareholder value and bonuses has destroyed the savings and pensions of the many while institutional investors have taken powers away from boards of directors. While all this has been going on, people have watched the 'soaps' and reality television and not questioned what has been happening.

Business schools have their responsibility too. Booz and Company (2008) describe what business schools have been teaching as a 'rules-plus-analytics' model. They explain how the model describes the rules governing corporate behaviour as constraints to be overcome, and provides analytical tools to work within or around these rules for the purpose of winning. Booz and Company argue: 'This model emphasizes impersonal aggressiveness in which managers walk as close to the legal and ethical line as possible – even crossing over it when they expect they won't get caught.'

A study from the Aspen Institute covering 2,000 graduates from the top 13 business schools in the United States found that business school education 'not only fails to improve the moral character of students, it actually weakens it' (Aspen Institute, 2002). We elevate these professional managers, with their MBAs, to positions of authority and they become harder and harder to challenge. These individuals have learned to manipulate forms of measurement. Checks and balances, corporate governance, self-regulatory bodies, have not worked and so we are where we are today.

Without these checks being effective, leaders develop over time the 'hubris effect', which is wonderfully demonstrated in the film *The Iron Lady*. When this occurs the strengths of the leaders become their weaknesses, resulting in confidence changing to arrogance; purpose becomes obsession, and perseverance becomes dogma and intransigence. The 'heroic' leaders start to overestimate their abilities and popularity; they discourage questions and may ridicule anyone who challenges them. In corporate takeovers these leaders often overestimate the bid, putting the whole process in jeopardy. This behaviour is not leadership as these individuals won't take responsibility or listen; they replace people who criticize them and regard themselves as above the rules.

Is it inevitable that the role of positional leader results in hubris? Research shows the answer is no. Reverence and respect of others is fundamental to the practice of leadership and should be part of leadership learning and development. When hubris occurs, individuals lose their sense of self and compassion; they reject responsibility and deny failures; they narrow their definition of success and use maladaptive coping skills that shut them off from their colleagues. Most of all they shut off all learning and become fixed. It is interesting that while employees are encouraged to learn and develop, executives often refuse with 'I'm too busy' and 'I already know all I need to know to do this job.' Positional leaders have a problem. Not only are they in danger of shutting themselves off from learning but they also have a negative impact on the leadership development of others.

We know that one of the key ways people learn leadership is by observing those in leader positions. In addition, Beverley Alimo-Metcalf made a study (2010) across public and private organizations of why leadership initiatives in organizations failed. She found the main barrier was the attitude of the most senior managers:

- There was reluctance to participate in such initiatives themselves, with top managers believing they had little need for new learning but that lower levels of managers did need such development.

- Within the organizations there was a strong awareness among middle managers of a lack of appropriate role models among the top executives, and this almost destroyed the potential benefits of investment to the organizations.

- There was no support from the top managers for proposals made by the managers who had participated in leadership programmes. This resulted in increased cynicism at lower levels in the organization, and enthusiasm resulting from the initiative died.

In other words, the lack of learning at positional leader level is creating a huge barrier to leadership. With cynicism throughout organizations, people won't engage, change becomes impossible and not only are the leaders stuck but the organization is stuck.

Leadership has to challenge the predominant management mindset that has risen to the top of organizations. Back in 2004 Henry Mintzberg concluded: 'conventional MBA programmes train the wrong people, in the wrong ways, with the wrong consequences'. He goes on to say that prestigious business schools are so obsessed with numbers and the drive to make management a science that they are damaging the discipline of management. He believes these universities should enrol more practising managers rather than postgraduate students with little experience, and use action learning and insights from their *own* problems and experiences rather than lectures on theories or case studies.

Universities in the United States, including Harvard, where many of the people who created the near financial collapse of the Western world graduated, are now taking a hard look at themselves, focusing on their original core purpose and changing. Leadership education is growing at a fast pace and with it the teachings of moral, reverent values.

On the day of the assassination in Dallas of JF Kennedy, the President was to make an important speech. Within that speech were the words: 'Leadership and learning are indispensable to each other.' These unspoken words need to be shouted today from all pillars of society.

The cry now is for leadership not leaders. What does this mean? In my research with young pupils in schools (Owen, 2007), it became clear that from the age of six or seven boys and girls differentiated between leader and leadership. A leader was older, bigger, bossy and cleverer. Leadership was about being honest, including people, being fair and courageous. The two concepts were understood as totally different. This differentiation became stronger as the children grew older. They also believed that leadership was learned. In other words, young people understand this, yet we rarely listen to them.

It is hoped that by exploring leadership from an international perspective we may be able to at least understand what has happened, whether the leadership crisis is a global issue and whether other factors are finding their way to the surface to address what sometimes feels like a lost generation and complex problems. Is leadership as a concept evolving with the rest of the world?

In Part I of this book, Professor Keith Grint explores whether the leadership we get is our enemy, using the example of Ibsen's play *An Enemy of the People*. He suggests that people are allergic to collaborative decision making in addressing complex issues and prefer a more 'commanding' style from one person. Is this true? Loren Fox (2003), in his study of the collapse of Enron, blames everyone on the board, not just the three who were held responsible. He asks why a board that included two former energy regulators, four executives from financial and investment firms and a professor in accountancy could not see the problems in the company's accountancy practices and speak up. Keith Grint tries to explain why these phenomena are happening. But is he right when he suggests that while leadership is desired, we return to commandship? Or is something else required before leadership is effective?

From India, Sangeeth Varghese takes us back in time as a way to explain why we are where we are today. He shows how organizations, and in particular the corporate world, have yet to catch up with other democratic organizations. It is a wonderful story we can all learn from. Is this why leaders today remain hierarchical and dominant?

Professor Elena Antonacopoulou shows that there needs to be a shift from 'leader' to 'leadership in practice'. She explains how ordinary people can do extraordinary things by practising their leadership in the real world. Her emphasis is the 'ship' of leadership and she literally relates it to a famous ship. She asks why so few people express leadership when a world cries out for it.

Is the problem that most people reject the 'label' of leader? Dr Tracey Manning addresses this issue and explains why so few people even want to be associated with leadership. As an academic psychologist with many years of research she highlights these key issues. In my own research in the UK with young people (Owen, 2007) it was found that the main reason over half of young people rejected leadership was the belief that 'I'm not good enough.' Is the problem that we look for the 'perfect' leader, the 'heroic' and charismatic individual, even in children?

Dr Fiona Kennedy was perplexed by a question from a delegate on a leadership programme she was facilitating. He was questioning whether what they were learning was about personal development. Dr Kennedy's chapter is a wonderful exploration of the assumptions we make when it comes to developing leadership, and follows on from the previous chapter. It shows that there are different ways of looking at leadership and the development of leadership.

The second part of the book shows that there is in the world today a transformation of leadership itself. Whereas Part I tackles some of the problems and challenges, Part II demonstrates what is actually happening in different parts of the world. Bridging the two parts is a short conversation with one of the most prestigious leadership writers of our time, Distinguished Professor Warren Bennis. It has been wonderful to include here a conversation with one of the world's best thinkers on leadership. Known for his research and work, he has supported many in the field of understanding leadership. Now in his mid-eighties and still writing and teaching, he explains his own leadership journey, which he describes as 'engaging with others'. Can we find different examples of this in parts of the world? Is this 'engaging with others' exactly how leadership is developing as a concept and practice?

Part II begins with Jesus Sampedro Hidalgo, who shows how leadership itself is evolving in South America. With this region becoming a strong economic force it is interesting to see the shift developing away from the individual leader.

Likewise, it is wonderful to include China. Here, Professor Jiacheng Li explains the journey of leadership in education and schools for a fast-changing society. When I visited the University in Shanghai last year, the assumption was that I would bring knowledge, but I learned so much more from the professors. It is that sharing of knowledge that is the aim of this book and an essential part of leadership in the 21st century. At the University in China the mission was clearly engraved in stone: Seek Truth, Foster Originality, and Live Up to the Name of Teacher.

Perhaps what is needed *is* a leadership crisis in the West to challenge the philosophy of the 'individual' that has led us to an economic crisis affecting so many. What we cannot escape is the near collapse of the Western economic world. The protesters' tents may have been moved from St Paul's Cathedral but the issues have not gone away. Brian Patterson gives an honest, up-to-date account of the rise and fall of the Irish economy and the impact this is having on leadership. He shows with clarity the challenges the Western world is facing. It appears to be affecting and changing the leadership people are now engaging in and is a shift away from what we see at the beginning of the book. It turns out that this book is a story of hope. Like leadership, this book has become a journey: a journey around the world that clearly shows how leadership is adapting. New thinking on leadership is not the prerogative just of academics but of everyday people.

Here is an attempt to bring new insights and thinking on leadership from around the world that may enable practitioners and academics to try and turn around what has been called 'the leadership crisis'. At times the book is controversial; at other times new understanding from different fields of research are included that together give a global picture of where our understanding of leadership is today and where it is heading. Leadership is an unlimited resource and as such, is a lifelong pursuit of learning. That learning must be to transform 'leader of position' to 'leadership with moral purpose'. When our so-called leaders realize that they are in their roles to first serve people, rather than the other way around, we should see that the problems and challenges in the world can and must be resolved. Then the pursuit of leadership will be for all of us, not just the few.

References

Alimo-Metcalfe, B and Alben-Metcalfe, J (2010) Leadership in the public sector and third sector organisations, in *Leadership in Organisations*, 2nd edn, ed John Storey, Routledge, London

Aspen Institute (2002) *Beyond Grey Pinstripes*, Aspen Institute

Booz and Company (2008) *Strategy and Business*, 51 (Summer)

Fox, L (2003) *Enron: The Rise and Fall*, John Wiley, New York

Mintzberg, H (2004) *Managers not MBAs*, Barrett-Koehler, San Francisco

Owen, H (2007) *Creating Leaders in the Classroom*, Routledge, London

Work Foundation (2009) *Developing Leaders*, The Work Foundation, 30 March

Part I
Challenges for
leadership

Is leadership the enemy of the people?[1]

01

KEITH GRINT

Introduction

In Ibsen's play *An Enemy of the People*, Stockmann is the Norwegian town doctor who tries to persuade the citizens that its new public baths (designed to bring in much-needed business from tourists) have been contaminated and must be closed. The people, therefore, must take collective responsibility for protecting tourists by admitting the problem and sacrificing their financial gain for the greater good. In the event the town scapegoats Stockmann for his audacity and ostracizes him. Here is captured the precise nature of the problem of leadership – defined as engaging the collective in facing up to its collective problems. Leaders are not heroic knights on horseback rescuing damsels in distress; they are instead more likely to be Stockmannesque figures, fighting both their own demons and the smallminded nature of their neighbours. This is necessary work, but it is not heroic because, as the title reminds us, often leadership is not perceived by the people as for the people but against them, often configured as part of the Cassandra complex – the person who can foresee the future but whose message is anathema to those that need to hear it. Indeed, leadership here might well be 'the enemy of the people'.

This chapter considers the extent to which we remain allergic to 'leadership', which is the collaborative decision style appropriate for addressing collective complex problems, and more favourably inclined towards, if not actually addicted to, 'command': that is, the decisive decision making appropriate to a 'commander' in a crisis. The latter is achieved by configuring the world as one of permanent crises, where the only viable responses are decisive commands. Of course some people configure the world as one full of 'Tame Problems', where the only viable responses are to keep rolling out the same process that normally works but that this time has led you into a recalcitrant problem. And there are some who see 'Wicked Problems' everywhere, where the only viable response is to delay decision making while you engage in yet more consultation and collaboration. These three responses are actually ideal types in the Weberian sense, rather than empirically common processes, but the typology is a useful way to open up the debate. That is, they are archetypal tendencies not iron laws, but nevertheless they remain extraordinarily difficult to displace. Of course, not every situation is a crisis or is constituted as a crisis by the decision makers, but this tendency to assume that most things either are crises, or don't get addressed until they become crises, seems particularly appropriate in the current climate and as a backdrop to our apparent inability to address very complex issues in any way other than through command and control. The next section considers a development of Rittell and Weber's (1973) original Tame and Wicked Problem typology as a way of establishing why this tendency has serious consequences.

Tame, Wicked and Critical Problems

Management and leadership, as two forms of authority rooted in the distinction between certainty and uncertainty, can be related to Rittell and Webber's (1973) typology of Tame and Wicked Problems (Grint, 2008). A Tame Problem may be complicated but is resolvable through unilinear acts and it is likely to have occurred before. In other words, there is only a limited degree of uncertainty and thus it is associated with management. Tame Problems are akin to puzzles – for which there is always an answer. The (scientific) manager's role, therefore, is to provide the appropriate process to solve the problem. A Wicked Problem is more complex, rather than just complicated – that is, it cannot be removed from its environment, solved and returned without affecting the environment. Moreover, there is no clear relationship between cause and effect. Such problems are often intractable – for instance, trying to develop a health service on the basis of a scientific approach (assuming it was a Tame Problem) would suggest providing everyone with all the services and medicines they required, based only on their medical needs. However, with an ageing population and an increasing medical ability to intervene and maintain life, we have a potentially infinite increase in demand but a finite level of economic resource, so there cannot be a scientific or medical or Tame solution to the problem of the National Health Service (NHS). In sum we cannot provide everything for everybody; at some point we need to make a political decision about who gets what and based on what criteria. This inherently contested arena is typical of a Wicked Problem. If we think about the NHS as the NIS – the National Illness Service – then we have a different understanding of the problem because it is essentially a series of Tame Problems: fixing a broken leg is the equivalent of a Tame Problem: there is a scientific solution and medical professionals in hospitals know how to fix them. But if you run (sorry, crawl) into a restaurant for your broken leg to be fixed it becomes a Wicked Problem because it's unlikely that anyone there will have the knowledge or the resources to fix it. Thus the category of problems is subjective not objective – what kind of a problem you have depends on where you are sitting and what you already know.

Moreover, many of the problems that the NHS deals with – obesity, drug abuse, violence – are not simply problems of health; they are often deeply complex social problems that sit across and between different government departments and institutions, so attempts to treat them through a single institutional framework are almost bound to fail. Indeed, because there are often no 'stopping' points with Wicked Problems – that is the point at which the problem is solved (eg there will be no more crime because we have solved it) – we often end up having to admit that we cannot solve Wicked Problems. Conventionally, we associate leadership with precisely the opposite: the ability to solve problems, act decisively and to know what to do. But we cannot know how to solve Wicked Problems, and therefore we need to be very wary of acting decisively precisely because we cannot know what will happen. If we knew what to do it would be a Tame Problem not a Wicked Problem. Yet the pressure to act decisively often leads us to try to solve the problem as if it was a Tame Problem. When global warming first emerged as a problem some of the responses concentrated on solving the problem through science (a Tame response), manifested in the development of biofuels; but we now know that the first generation of biofuels appear to have denuded the world of significant food resources so that what looked like a solution actually became another problem. Again, this is typical of what happens when we try to solve Wicked Problems: other problems emerge to compound the original problem. So we can make things better or worse – we can drive our cars slower and less or faster and more – but we may not be able to solve global warming; we may just have to learn to live with a different world and make the best of it we can. In other words, we cannot start again and design a perfect future – though many political and religious extremists might want us to.

The 'we' in this is important because it signifies the importance of the collective in addressing Wicked Problems. Tame Problems might have individual solutions in the sense that an individual is likely to know how to deal with it. But since Wicked Problems are partly defined by the absence of an answer on the part of the leader, it behoves the individual leader to ask the right kind of questions to engage the collective in an attempt to come to terms with the problem. In other words, Wicked Problems require the transfer of authority from individual to collective because only collective engagement can hope to address the problem. The uncertainties involved in Wicked Problems imply that leadership, as I am defining it, is not a science but an art – the art of engaging a community in facing up to complex collective problems.

Examples of Wicked Problems would include: developing a transport strategy, or a response to global warming, or a response to anti-social behaviour, or a national health system. Wicked Problems are not necessarily rooted in longer time frames than Tame Problems, because an issue that appears to be Tame or Critical can often be turned into a (temporary) Wicked Problem by delaying the decision. For example, President Kennedy's actions during the Cuban Missile Crisis were often based on asking questions of his civilian assistants that required some time for reflection – despite the pressure from his military advisers to provide instant answers. Had Kennedy accepted the advice of the American Hawks we would have seen a third set of problems that fall outside the Wicked/Tame dichotomy – a Critical Problem, in this case probably a nuclear war. However, reframing a problem as Wicked can also be used as an excuse for inactivity when actually a decision is required. This is particularly appropriate for the third set of problems, which I will refer to as Critical.

A Critical Problem, such as a 'crisis', is presented as self-evident in nature, as allowing very little time for decision making and action, and it is often associated with authoritarianism. Here there is virtually no uncertainty – at least in the behaviour of the commander, whose role is to take the required decisive action – about what needs to be done: that is, to provide the answer to the problem, not to engage standard operating procedures or SOPs (management) if these delay the decision – or to ask questions (leadership).

Translated into Critical Problems, I suggest that for such crises we do need decision makers who are god-like in their decisiveness and their ability to provide the answer to the crisis. And since we reward people who are good in crises – and ignore people who are such good managers that there are very few crises – commanders soon learn to seek out (or reframe situations as) crises. Of course, it may be that the commander remains privately uncertain about whether the action is appropriate or the presentation of the situation as a crisis is persuasive, but that uncertainty will probably not be apparent to his or her followers.

Defining these three forms of authority – Command, Management and Leadership – is, in turn, another way of suggesting that the role of those responsible for decision making is to find the appropriate Answer, Process and Question, respectively, in order to address the problem. This is not meant as a discrete typology but a heuristic device to enable us to understand why those charged with decision making sometimes appear to act in ways that others find incomprehensible. Thus I am not suggesting that the correct decision-making process lies in the correct analysis of the situation – that would be to generate a deterministic approach – but I am suggesting that decision makers tend to legitimize their actions on the basis of a persuasive account of the situation. In short, the social construction of the problem legitimizes the deployment of a particular form of authority. Take, for example, the current situation of public finances. Many countries are mired in debates about which public expenditure to cut and which – if any – to protect. Indeed, politicians of all varieties seem to be falling over themselves to acquire the commander's mantle to inflict pain upon the apparently profligate public sector wasters of our tax revenues. But this is to mistake the cause for the effect – the cause of the problem is the profligate investment bankers not the parsimonious public sector employees! Moreover, it is often the case that the same individual or group with authority will switch between the command, management and leadership roles as they perceive – and constitute – the problem as Critical, Tame or Wicked, or even as a single problem that itself shifts across these boundaries. Indeed, this movement – often perceived as 'inconsistency' by the decision makers' opponents – is crucial to success as the situation, or at least our perception of it, changes.

That persuasive account of the problem partly rests in the decision makers' access to – and preference for – particular forms of power, and herein lies the irony of 'leadership': it remains the most difficult of approaches and one that many decision makers will often try to avoid at all costs – another reason why an addiction to command appears so commonplace.

The notion of 'power' suggests that we need to consider how different approaches to, and forms of, power fit with this typology of authority, and

FIGURE 1.1 Typology of problems, power and authority

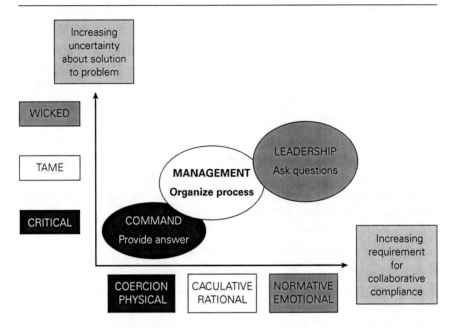

amongst the most useful for our purposes is Etzioni's (1964) typology of compliance, which distinguished between coercive, calculative and normative compliance. Coercive or physical power was related to total institutions, such as prisons or armies; calculative compliance was related to 'rational' institutions, such as companies; and normative compliance was related to institutions or organizations based on shared values, such as clubs and professional societies. This compliance typology fits well with the typology of problems: Critical Problems are often associated with coercive compliance; Tame Problems are associated with calculative compliance; and Wicked Problems are associated with normative compliance – you cannot force people to follow you in addressing a Wicked Problem because the nature of the problem demands that followers have to want to help.

This typology can be plotted along the relationship between two axes. as shown in Figure 1.1, with the vertical axis representing increasing uncertainty about the solution to the problem – in the behaviour of those in authority – and the horizontal axis representing the increasing need for collaboration in resolving the problem.

Addicted to command and allergic to leadership

The issue of addiction is particularly problematic with regard to Wicked Problems because these tend to be the most serious, at least in the long run, and because most of our leaders seem to have a preference for treating Wicked Problems as Critical Problems, requiring a coercive response from a commander. Perhaps the point is not to insist that no problem is critical – a crisis – or that they are all Wicked and therefore collaborative leadership is always necessary, or they are Tame so we just need to manage the scientific standard operating procedures (SOPs) – but to use the apparent crisis to make the collective face up to their collective responsibilities. In effect, to launch the collective processes associated with Wicked Problems on the back of the limited stability derived from command. But since we are often addicted to seeing problems as crises we tend to prefer temporary bouts of command 'solutions' to all kinds of Wicked Problems that can only really be addressed by long-term collaborative engagements. So, for example, we see the problem of knife crime addressed as a crisis with various uncoordinated and short-term command responses (more stop-and-search or longer prison sentences based on 'three hits and out' and so on), all of which usually fail. In contrast, the only effective responses seem to be those that treat the problem as a short-term crisis that generates the impetus to reconfigure the problem as Wicked, which requires a long-term collaborative engagement by the whole community. The trick here, then, is to ask the right question. Not, 'How do we stop knife crime?' but 'How do we get the community more involved in self-policing?'

This implies not that commanders are irrelevant but that they are critical in the development of the conditions for persuading people first to pay attention to the problem and subsequently to enact an appropriate response to a Wicked Problem; thus only through the careful construction of a 'crisis' can leadership be deployed to address a Wicked Problem effectively. The problems, if we are addicted to crisis, are: first, that in shifting from one decision mode to the other we are often accused of being inconsistent in a situation (in effect we need to be managers, leaders and commanders at different times); second, that the addiction to command is not restricted to power-hungry commanders but also involves anxiety-prone and responsibility-avoiding followers; third, that getting off the addiction will require the equivalent of 'cold turkey', the unpleasant period of 'drying out' so that the addiction is gradually halted. Instant cold turkey can be as fatal as the initial addiction.

That we are in a permanent crisis seems commonplace. Indeed, there has been a flurry of publications recently that have used the term 'crisis' and 'permanent' as a starting point. Heifetz, Grashow and Linsky (2009), for example, have argued that 'today's mix of urgency, high stakes and uncertainty will continue as the norm even after the recession ends'. As a consequence they argue that we should 'foster adaptation', embrace the disequilibrium that will provide just enough pressure on followers to accept the necessary changes, and maximize the opportunities for people to experience leadership by supporting organizational experiments. All this is because we are allegedly facing a crisis of a different category than before – a 'permanent crisis' in which the old ways must be replaced by new ones. That includes replacing our normal response to crisis, which is avoiding the causes and merely treating the symptoms. In the public sectors of all European countries this would manifest itself in establishing what services should *not* be provided by the public services, rather than simply finding more efficient ways to cut budgets. Of course, whether we are living in an era of permanent crisis is highly debatable and always contestable, but the nature of 'the situation' (Grint, 2005) is less relevant here than the causes of this common assumption; so why do we assume this?

First, there is an issue that relates to the fear of failure, which itself derives from the fear of freedom. When leaders and managers make an error of judgement they are not usually forgiven their human frailties but dragged through the proverbial public streets on symbolic tumbrels. As Durkheim (1973) argued, many followers like to perceive their leaders as gods – omnipotent, omniscient and flawed; so when the inevitable error occurs, those same followers that hailed the leader as a god can then have the satisfaction of watching the public execution of the person who 'betrayed' their trust. The result is an abject fear of responsibility, manifest most clearly in the response of politicians and public service managers when, for example, children are murdered while being known to the social services. We might usefully turn to Erich Fromm's (1942) *Fear of Freedom* to pursue this a little further, for he argues that we have an almost compulsive submission to authority as a result of modernity, which has uprooted people from communal relationships and generated an intolerable loneliness and consequent weight of responsibility. This fear drives us to seek solace in the protective arms of authority, either fascist or democratic, because only in that way can we avoid the fear generated by personal responsibility. This, in another context, is what Bauman (1993) calls, 'the unbearable silence of responsibility'. Of course, this also implies that arguments about the 'death of deference' are much exaggerated, and one only has to consider the response of fans to celebrities, monarchists to the royal family, or believers to their gods, to recognize that deference is still alive and kicking, even if the form may have changed.

Second, it is often in the interests of the media to portray situations as crises in order to sell more copy and thus induce higher levels of advertisements. The swine fever 'crisis' in the summer of 2009 was one example: on 25 July 2009 the UK's *Daily Express* predicted that the fever would bring the British National Health Service to its knees. It didn't. In fact fewer people seem to have died of swine flu than the normal seasonal flu – but that didn't stop the paper predicting the end of the medical world in the UK. Similarly, although we are regularly assailed with tales of imminent mass destruction at the hands of terrorists, according to the *World Health Report* (2008), the numbers of people killed by terrorists in the world each year is usually numbered in the hundreds, while the numbers killed in road traffic accidents, through smoking, via HIV/Aids or even diarrhoea are in the millions. 'The War on Diarrhoea' does not make the newspaper headlines, even though 'The War on Terror' regularly does. But we cannot simply blame the media for this – if we did not buy their products they wouldn't be able to function in this way. So whatever 'they' do, 'we' are part of the problem.

Third, it may be that there is something about our love of excitement, our addiction to adrenalin, which conditions us to perceive many situations as crises. Thus our attempt to get beyond the mundaneness of everyday life propels us to escape into romantic fantasies of crisis and heroism. The double-headed nature of celebrity also occupies this space: we herald the new football manager or political leader – such as Barack Obama – as the charismatic messiah and are then surprised when they turn out to have what some might call feet of clay. We can also see this effect in the rash of 'instant leadership' books: if you have not achieved significant changes in the first 90 days then you are self-evidently a failure.

Fourth, our attempts to distance ourselves from what Meindl, Ehrlich and Dukerich (1985) called, 'the Romance of [Heroic] Leadership' seems to have led many to assume that some form of distributed leadership through partnership working is the solution to all our problems. But the evidence thus far suggests that distributed leadership is anything but a simple solution to a complex problem (Leonard, 2010) and the subsequent difficulties of making it work seem to have led many to resort to command and control in the face of collective congealment and indecision. In effect we seem to have replaced the romance of heroic leadership with the romance of distributed leadership and discovered that neither seems viable.

Finally, we seem to have a problem with Nietzschean anxiety over the determination of causation. In other words, when situations appear both threatening and ambiguous we seem to demand a clear causal agency; because if we cannot establish this agency then 'the problem' is potentially irresolvable. Thus, for example, in Scott Snook's (2002) *Friendly Fire* (on the accidental shooting down of US Blackhawks in Iraq), his conclusion is not that the pilots of the US fighters were to blame, or that the Blackhawk pilots were to blame, or that the 'system' was to blame, but that it was impossible to determine who or what was to blame – there was 'no bad guy... no smoking gun, no culprit'. In the presence of such a conclusion the tendency seems to be to dismiss the report and to find 'the culprit' by looking harder, not to accept the conclusion. In short, such intolerable Nietzschean anxiety guides us back into the search for a commander to resolve the irresolvable crisis.

Conclusion

Our predilection for crisis and command often undermines our attempts to address Wicked Problems, despite 'leadership' being the most appropriate decision style for these. In contrast, 'leadership', defined as persuading the collective to take responsibility for collective problems (while still recognizing that part of the role of leaders is to shoulder a disproportionate amount of that responsibility), is often regarded not just as difficult and dangerous, but as 'the enemy of the people'. Is this why leadership is so difficult? Just when we need it, decision makers step back not from but towards the brink; from an assumption rooted in a Wicked Problem to an assumption rooted in a Critical Problem; from leadership to command.

Note

1   A version of this chapter first appeared in *The International Journal of Leadership in Public Services*, 6 (4), November 2010.

References

Bauman, Z (1993) *Postmodern Ethics*, Blackwell, Oxford

Durkheim, E (1973) 1883 address to the Lycéen of Sans, in *Emile Durkheim on Morality and Society*, ed RN Bellah, pp 25–33, University of Chicago Press, Chicago

Etzioni, A (1964) *Modern Organizations*, Prentice Hall, London

Fromm, E (1942) *The Fear of Freedom*, Routledge, London

Grint, K (2005) Problems, problems, problems, problems: the social construction of leadership, *Human Relations* 58, pp 1467–94

Grint, K (2008) Wicked Problems and clumsy solutions: the role of leadership, *Clinical Leader*, 1 (2), pp 54–68

Heifetz, R, Grashow, A and Linsky, M (2009) Leadership in a (permanent) crisis, *Harvard Business Review*, July–August, p 3

Leonard, P (2010) *The Romance of Collaborative Leadership*, Unpublished PhD thesis, Lancaster University

Meindl, JR, Ehrlich, SB and Dukerich, JM (1985) The romance of leadership, *Administrative Science Quarterly*, 30, pp 78–102

Rittell, H and Webber, M (1973) Dilemmas in a general theory of planning, *Policy Sciences*, 4, pp 155–69

Snook, SA (2002) *Friendly Fire*, Princeton University Press, Princeton, NJ

World Health Report, 2008 [Online] http://www.who.int/whr/2008/en/index.html (accessed 28 April 2012)

Totalitarianism to democracy

02

Why would today's closed organizations evolve towards democratic structures?

SANGEETH VARGHESE

Why modern day politicians share the same DNA as bandits and crooks

In the beginning, there were a bunch of thieves, crooks and promiscuous chaps. Everything good in the world that we know of today – our democratic governments, egalitarian societies and free market system – started out with the above.

Mancur Lloyd Olson, the celebrated American political scientist, in his final book *Power and Prosperity* (2000), told us the interesting story of a bunch of bandits who, during the initial days of human settlement, roamed around villages plundering, killing and raping. When one of these bandits struck a village, he took everything with little regard for the future. However, many of them soon started to encounter a couple of perplexing problems. The first one was, as people in these communities were never too sure when another bandit would pass by and steal their wealth, they had no real incentive to work hard or save their produce. Hence, they started working less, earning just enough for their daily sustenance and living more by the day. Bandits were surprised that their source of wealth was increasingly drying out with each visit. The second problem was the competition that they started to face in their profession. With time, there were quite a few bandits, and hence a 'roving bandit', as Olson called him, was never too sure that another bandit would not have served himself the next time he comes around.

Roving bandits grew smarter. They eventually realized that it made more sense for them to settle down in a village than roam around. The reasoning behind this was simple. A 'stationary bandit' could exploit his victims over a longer term and hence had more security about his own future and the resources that he had access to. However, as they settled down, these bandits realized that a stationary life was quite different from a roving one. Plunder was redefined as taxation, but taxes had to be kept within a realistic limit since overexploitation, they realized, killed the source of their future revenue. They grabbed their subject's incomes for themselves only up to a point where reduced incentives led to diminished tax returns. A stationary bandit set tax rates at a level that maximized his revenue; since the incentive for a villager to produce more fell as taxes rose, the bandit maximized his revenue at a tax rate far lower than 100 per cent.

Slowly, the stationary bandit's life took another surprising turn. The realization came to him that it was to his interest that he not only did not overexploit his people, but also invested in their welfare. He had a stake in that village, and hence if it prospered, he could extract more for himself in taxes and other ways. So in the short term, a stationary bandit kept taxes low, while in the medium term he started providing growth, promoting public goods like infrastructure and transportation, both of which promoted domestic growth, which further increased his revenues. He invested a part of the tax money also in defence, to protect himself as well as the villagers from the onslaught of roving bandits.

However, these investments in public goods also depended on the confidence of the stationary bandit about his power. The more confident he was of continued reign, the more interest he would have in the welfare of his people, because then the economy would be strong enough to keep him rich for as long as he was is in power. The longer the time horizons assured for the bandit, the more his interests approached those of his people, so, of the forms of government where the ruled had no choice of ruler, hereditary rulers were a better prospect. These bandits eventually created hereditary kingdoms to assure their continued rule and transformed themselves into totalitarian and autocratic rulers.

So, through history, bandits realized that it was better to settle down and invest in the welfare of a community, while people realized that it was better to live under political tyranny than to be subject to the depredations of roving bandits. Advancing from the latter to the former condition marked the start of civilization and laid the foundations of modern day nation states.

Now the question is, how did democracy evolve from these totalitarian empires set up by stationary bandits? Authors Daron Acemoglu and James Robinson think they have an answer. In their book *Economic Origins of Dictatorship and Democracy* (2006), they wrote that in typical societies there are two kinds of people – elites (in a totalitarian set-up, they are the autocratic ruler and his set of relatives and cronies) and citizens. 'While, totalitarianism is the rule by the elite, democracy rule is by numerous groups, who constitute the majority, ie the citizens.' In totalitarianism, elites get the policies that they want, while in democracy the citizens have more power to get what they want. Since the elites lose under democracy they naturally have an incentive to oppose or subvert it. Yet, surprisingly, most democracies arise when they are created by the elites.

So, why does a totalitarian ever democratize? Interestingly, according to the authors, democratic values and institutions did not arise as a direct contradiction of totalitarian forms of governance. Rather, they emerged by a gradual shift in the distribution of power in society. Through time, as a totalitarian made concessions, through lower tax rates, provision of public goods and firmer property rights (primarily to serve his own interests of wealth maximization), that actually resulted in citizens gaining more power and voice. This shift created a movement towards a more balanced relationship between the rights and interests of the citizens and of the totalitarian.

Through an eventual accumulation of the rights given away by the totalitarian, citizens reached a position where they could even threaten the totalitarian force to make them concessions. These threats took the form of strikes, demonstrations, riots or even revolutions. Since these threats imposed a cost on the totalitarian, and to his interests, he wanted to prevent them. He could do so either by repression, concessions or as a last step by giving away political power. But, repression was always so costly that it was not an attractive option. Hence, the totalitarian often bought off the citizens with promises of policy concessions, such as income redistribution and more stable property rights, rather than conceding a real transfer of power.

However, as rational actors themselves, even citizens cared about their future. As forward-looking economic actors, they not only cared about economic allocations of today, but about the future. They understood that though they gained some policy concessions, it was still easy for the total-itarian to renege on any of these. Anticipating this, citizens were still unsatis-fied and chose to revolt, leaving the totalitarian with no option but to reduce his power by transferring authority to the citizens. He was compelled to build up democratic institutions that were harder to reverse and that guaranteed long-term success to the citizens. So, in fact the totalitarian was forced to democratize – create a credible commitment to future majoritarian policies, if he wished to avoid more radical outcomes.

A research paper titled, 'Social origins of democracy' written by Jayashree Viswanathan (2006) demonstrates this real-time evolution in the case of one of the older and most successful democracies of the world – England.

> During the 5th century AD, following the fall of the Roman Empire, England came under constant barbarian invasions. With the shadows of unpredictable attacks looming over them, people lived under constant fear, insecurity and poverty. Eventually, as a few warlords found advantage in settling down, people quickly surrendered their lands and labour in return for shelter and support. The quest for physical security resulted in economic subjection and military allegiance to these stationary bandits, which eventually gave rise to a tightly hierarchical feudal system.

By the dawn of the 11th century, the cessation of attacks from barbarian invaders and the stability of the feudal system provided a sense of physical security to the people, enabling them to channel their energy towards the revival of agriculture. By the 15th century, one force, the monarch, consolidated his authority compared to the other feudal lords, resulting in the steady growth of the nation state. The Divine Right propaganda, which was unleashed, claim-ing the monarch as the representative of God on earth, ensured continuity of power, enabling him to take a greater interest in his people's welfare.

Increased welfare strengthened the liberalizing forces in the agrarian society, where people started aspiring for more economic freedom. The rise of money economy and shift from a subsistence economy to a market economy intensified these aspirations, as feudalism was gradually replaced by a newly wealthy merchant class. Through the 16th and 17th centuries, these changes continued, where there was a massive shift of wealth away from the monarch, and from the very rich, towards the middle class. This section of society became the forces of change and fought against the conservative hierarchical order of society. They clamoured for more rights – rights to trade freely and for freedom of expression. 'For the first time in history, men were demanding something more from the State than merely law and order and security against foreign enemies,' says Will Durant (1993).

Meanwhile, stimulation of the national education system added teeth to this struggle. Secular education broadened men's outlook and sowed the seeds of political freedom. Ancient forces of conservatism were pushed to the background and new ideas of democracy and equality flourished in an atmosphere of free discussion and debate, even as demands for parliamentary reform, including manhood suffrage, kept mounting. Ultimately, the financial and constitutional conflicts of the 17th century ended in the shift of power from the monarch to the parliament.

However, the struggle did not end there. It continued to redistribute the economic and political benefits to all sections of the society. This quest expressed itself in the realm of knowledge as the rise of modern science; in the field of economics as the rise of capitalism and money economy; in the sphere of industry as successive technological revolutions; and in the political sphere as democratic revolution and the progressive affirmation of individual human rights. These interrelated movements gradually led to the rising value of the individual in society and the spread of democratic institutions, enabling England to eventually establish one of the true democracies in the world at that point in time.

How did a rapist evolve into a doting father?

Not surprisingly, plundering was not the only thing that was in the minds of these bandits who roamed around during the initial days of human beings. Women were clearly another motive. As they attacked a village, they hunted out and mated with the best women around, often forcefully, before moving on to the next place. However, these powerful and dominant males, or roving bandits, were not exceptions. In fact, most other males did the same, travelling from place to place, as hunter-gatherers, sexually cohabiting with women of a place, before moving on. Eventually, as some of these roving rogues decided to settle in one place, to guard the wealth and women exclusively for themselves, they initiated a new way of living and a new way of livelihood – agriculture.

Men started increasingly to settle down in their farming communities, also marking drastic changes in their sexual lives. Relationships, until then casual and short, started to acquire a longer time horizon. While the bandit totalitarians maintained exclusive harems filled with the best women, often numbering thousands, lesser men held their women as common properties, where they enjoyed open sexual relationships. Women were treated as commodities and had no voice in the society or in the selection of their partners. Men forced themselves upon women, who being significantly smaller complied and submitted.

However, a man's dominion over multiple partners brought about a surprising twist. During hunter days, he could impregnate a woman and could move on with little thought of taking care of the offspring. In well-settled small agrarian communities, this was not possible. Men also had to provide for these children. In harems, which were exclusive in access, men were almost sure about their parenthood, while in open access communities they ended up providing for even those children whom they were not sure belonged to them. For a man, this meant his limited wealth, energy and efforts being invested in non-biological children, when they could ideally have been invested in raising his own.

Men slowly started resigning themselves to the fact that though holding multiple women as common property was a great proposition, monogamy, where one man exclusively cohabited with one woman, was more in their self-interest. Monogamy allowed them to invest their energy in bringing up their own children, and not someone else's. Marital relations started evolving at a faster pace.

However, there was still a problem that prevented a larger society from evolving. The bandit totalitarians. They had the money and wealth to sustain multiple women. Also, since they maintained exclusive access they were sure about the parenthood of the children they produced. Hence, they were least interested in a monogamous structure that limited them to one woman, whereas they could have multiple wives under polygyny. Evolutionary psychologist Santoshi Kanazawa has the answer. He says that in a society where a few men hold many women in their harems, most other men (especially the less powerful ones) would be left without mates simply because there are similar numbers of men and women in most societies. So, from a social standpoint, when there is resource inequality in a society (which there is in every human society), most men benefit more from monogamy than from polygyny, because it guarantees that every man can find a wife. Extremely powerful men do benefit from polygyny, but all other men benefit from monogamy. Hence, the popular pressure would always be to evolve towards monogamy.

However, this movement towards monogamy did not change the status of women in any manner. Men still behaved as despots in their families, overpowered women, and oppressed them with their childbearing and home-keeping responsibilities. Children, again, had no role, other than being obedient to the absolute patriarchal autocracy.

Through time, this new authority again started to undergo a transformation, as patriarchs started realizing that though their totalitarianism forced family members to behave in ways that they wanted, it also created a sense of resentment and antipathy, reducing the overall family happiness. They found that taking a genuine interest in their families' affairs and being benevolent brought in better results, satisfaction and contentment than ruling with an iron hand. Absolute authority slowly gave way to gentle authority, with patriarchs who understood that their power is the cornerstone of their family's well-being and sense of security.

These gentle authorities no longer needed to instil fear in order to communicate their influence. They still made rules, but fair ones and enforced them consistently. For the wife, and children, life with a gentle authority was more predictable and secure, guaranteeing them more freedom than had been possible until then. Moreover, during the late 17th century, a trend towards reduced size of many larger households changed the relationships between the members. They became more concerned about each other.

Moving into the 18th century, a real shift in family life took place, one that reflected a general social-cultural shift in human values and philosophy. With the emergence of the European Enlightenment, freedom, autonomy and individual rights became the dominant social ideals of the day, impacting all aspects of human life, including marriage. Increasingly, marriage came to be seen as a mutual choice of the couple entering into it, a choice based on love. People's expectations of marriage and family life also changed; love, romance and companionship became important considerations as well.

The spread of education, urbanization and feminism further intensified changes in family hierarchy. These opened up a greater variety of opportunities and occupations for women, thus affording them greater social power. With this, men's traditional role changed too. As wives assumed a larger role, they felt justified in demanding that husbands perform more childcare and housework. Men were also better prepared to move into this role, because by this time they were released from the burden of sole responsibility of supporting the family and hence had a better emotional connection with their children.

Children, meanwhile, were part of more caring families, had more educational opportunities than their parents ever had and enjoyed economic freedom, even at a younger age. These enabled them to demand more voice in the family affairs. Slowly, families moved towards true democracy, where everyone was regarded as an equal. Parents were no longer keeping their children in a state of virtual servitude. Disagreements were increasingly resolved through discussion, negotiation and compromise. Cooperation and harmony became hallmarks of a family.

So families, like nation states, evolved from a band of a few sexually promiscuous dominant males practising polygamy towards a totalitarian monogamy, eventually resulting in a democratic family that we see now.

Nation states evolved. Families evolved. But organizations refuse to do so

'A corporation is about the closest thing to a totalitarian institution that humans have ever contrived,' says Noam Chomsky (2010), the American linguist, philosopher and, most importantly, prominent cultural figure:

> We have had three forms of totalitarianisms in the 20th century: bolshevism, fascism and corporation. All three of these were characterized by a convergence of total power at the top, driving a hidden agenda, where people below were continuously suppressed, dominated, controlled and alienated through various means. The people at the top not only asserted themselves, but also constantly forbade and suppressed any criticism and opposition that went against their agenda. Two of these totalitarian forms, fortunately, dissolved and have disappeared mostly. But the third, the corporate sector, still remains.

Chomsky suggests that corporations, like the other totalitarian forms, are not accidental evolutions, but consciously designed to keep the power concentrated at the top. All the decision making lies with either the CEO or the board of directors or both, while orders are transmitted down to the lower levels, where complete subservience is expected. 'Unfortunately, at the lower levels, people have [agreed] to rent themselves to the corporation. They are called by different names and adorn different designations, but the truth is that there is not much of a difference between slavery and renting one's self to an owner, or to a "wage slavery"', comments Chomsky (2010).

In his paper 'Organizational totalitarianism and voices of dissent' (2007), Professor Howard Stein agrees with Chomsky. He says that the corporate world of today reflects a distinctive totalitarianism style similar to fascist attitudes and relationships of yesterday. For all those who would immediately jump to the defence of corporations, he brings in a caveat that not all totalitarian forms need look alike ideologically, because the real intentions would ultimately be revealed only through actions. Stein suggests that though in modern times most corporate leaders would not display the blatant aggressiveness of a Hitler or Mussolini, and in fact may pretend to be just the opposite, in due course they always show their true colours.

Stein reiterates his point by citing the example of Albert Dunlap, the former CEO of Scott Paper and then Sunbeam, who called himself 'Rambo in pinstripes'. Danlap earned the epithets 'Chainsaw Al' and 'The Shredder' by turning around troubled companies through relentless employee firings and numerous plant closures. As these names imply, he treated people as if they were inanimate things. The only people he ever cared about were his stockholders and the only thing the shareholder value. In his book, *Mean Business: How I save bad companies and make good companies great*, published in 1996, he polarized the world into shareholders (the good people, who were to be appeased) and workers (the bad people, who were disposable). In fact, Dunlap's compatriot Newton White once characterized Dunlap's approach to managing subordinates as: 'Piss all over them and then build them up.'

Jack Welch, who adorned America's loftiest executive perch for close to two decades, is probably the most appropriate example to understand the point that Stein is trying to make. Welch took over as GE's youngest-ever chairman and CEO in 1981, during a time of slow economic growth. The gloomy situation around would not deter him, already obsessed with shareholder value. Welch's resolution was to driving up the productivity in GE, by whatever means. He shut down factories, reduced payrolls and cut 'lackluster' old-line units, all the while pushing his theory that only shareholders mattered, and nothing else. Jack Welch was eventually crowned the Manager of the Century, and was celebrated across the media, not because he built a democratic institution – ironically in a country that vouched for its open values – but because he managed to build up a behemoth where totalitarian values were unashamedly practised and individual voices were blatantly squashed.

However, are these offbeat cases, blown out of proportions? We decided to ask a sample of 500 employees working in 190 large and medium-sized private corporations in three countries – the United States, UK and India. We made sure that our respondents were randomly drawn from across levels – lower, middle and senior (other than CEOs and board members) –

and across industries. The study was done through a short questionnaire, and guaranteed absolute confidentiality to the participants. Results would have hardly been surprising for Chomsky and Stein. Under 4 per cent of the total sample, including all of those belonging to the senior management cadre, claimed that they ever felt truly empowered to take decisions. Interestingly, a fifth of our respondents, at some point in their current company, tried to take their own decisions, but felt cheated as they were not given full organizational support. Most of them had to give up on their plans and make way for the orders from the top. Almost all of them felt that despite all the talk about democratic values and freedom in their organizations, their role was actually limited to carrying out the marching orders given by their seniors. None, absolutely none of these employees, irrespective of their levels of responsibility, and of the industries or nations that they came from, responded that they had absolute clarity about the strategic paths they took in their organizations.

Vijaya Menon, head of marketing (while this chapter was being written), at Kingfisher Red, a low-cost airline in India, worked under Vijay Mallya. Mallya, known as the glamour king of the Indian corporate sector, has styled himself on Richard Branson, splurging money on Formula 1 and an Indian Premier League cricket team. However, glamour ends right there, according to Vijaya. 'Mallya has managed to build a highly competitive and professional team, yet it is almost a dictatorial regime. In internal company meetings, when he is present, we have trained ourselves to meekly sit back and listen. He talks and no one else. Not even questions or doubts.' Vijaya specifically remembers a meeting where a new concept of Kingfisher airlines was being presented – a meeting attended by all high officials, including the Executive Vice President from the company supposedly in charge of everything. 'I expected that meeting to be different, but unfortunately there were no surprises. No one spoke except Mallya. He had this air about him that when I know everything, why should anyone else talk?' said Vijaya (2010).

Sandeep Bhargava is the CEO of Studio18, a large Bollywood studio in India. Sandeep says that his career is ridden with examples of companies that pride themselves on being professionally managed, but in reality control every aspect of decision making, even the less significant ones. Authority is firmly placed on the shoulders of one leader, who guards it. Sandeep challenges us to randomly pick any media organization in India, irrespective of whether they are television companies, advertising agencies, production houses or entertainment companies; they all exhibit the same pattern – they are rigorously driven by one personality or leader. So, there is always a

Subhash Ghai, a leading Bollywood movie director, or a Subroto Roy, owner of a media house, or an AG Krishnamurthy, chairman of an advertising agency, who not only are the towering personalities behind their businesses, but also are the central points where the smallest of small decisions are being taken. 'In these companies,' says Sandeep, 'designations – be it General Manager or Director – tend to be just designations, since all the decisions are made at a central point, which is not you anyway' (2010).

Ram Mynampatti, a whole-time director and briefly the interim CEO of the now notorious Satyam Computers, sums up the argument about totalitarianism in organizations well. In an interview given to a newspaper he said, 'Things were deliberately made so structured that no single leader in Satyam would ever get a complete picture of the company's performance at the operational level. Each of us would be privy to a small slice of the business, regardless of the size' (2009).

So, we come back to our discussion on totalitarianism, and realize that after all what Chomsky and Stein concluded about corporations is correct – that they are indeed totalitarian structures, similar to other oppressive systems like fascism. We further reiterate our conclusion by quickly comparing our modern day organizations against political scientist Theodore M Vestal's defining attributes of state authoritarianism, which he defines as concentrated power structures, in which power is generated and maintained by a repressive system that excludes all potential challengers.

Take these six questions to determine the 'democracy quotient' in your organization for yourself:

- Is leadership in your organization self-appointed or can employees displace them on a basis of free choice among competitors?
- Does the leader of your organization indulge in unregulated exercise of his/her power or can the employees control his or her authority legally?
- Does the leadership in your organization make strategic decisions behind closed doors, or are they arrived at by consensus?
- Do employees lack the freedom to question leadership decisions without fear of repercussions? Does the leadership in your organization stigmatize meaningful opposition?
- Are employees refused their basic civil liberties – liberties that defend and protect them against the tyrannies of a totalitarian leadership?
- Are employees unable to pursue interests of their own choice inside the organization, irrespective of whether the leadership likes it or not?

If the answer is 'Yes' to more than three questions, totalitarianism is where your organization falls. Three or fewer means it is inclined towards democracy.

Why do organizations refuse to evolve, even as the rest of the world is doing so?

How do we explain this totalitarianism in corporations? Why do some of the most intelligent and well-read people in the world, employed in modern day organizations, put up with this tyranny, where their talents and potential are suppressed to meet someone else's hidden agenda?

Thomas Malone, an organizational theorist from MIT in the United States, points in an interview to a preconceived assumption that we human beings carry around with us – we attribute conventional patterns to a central controlling point. We mistakenly assume that predictable results are possible only if there is someone to control the attempts to achieve them.

For example, as we see a flock of birds flying in close 'V' formation, we suppose the bird at the front of the 'V' is the leader of the flock. 'Not so,' Malone writes:

> In fact, the biologists who study bird behaviour now believe that all the birds
> in the flock are flying based on a set of simple rules about where they fly
> in relation to their neighbours and the air currents they field, resulting in a
> V-shaped formation. Moreover, if we watch the flock closely, we shall see that
> no one bird stays in front of the 'V' for long. The bird in front is not the leader
> at all: its position is more or less a random result of the way the birds fly (2004).

Michael Resnick, another professor from MIT, in his paper 'Beyond the centralized mindset' (1996), points us to the termites – tiny, but the master architects of the animal world, which construct giant mound-like nests rising more than 10 feet tall, on the plains of Africa. Inside the mounds are intricate networks of tunnels and chambers. Each termite colony has a queen, which we all naturally assume to be the leader. 'But, the termite queen does not "tell" the termite workers what to do,' writes Professor Resnick, who studies these colonies. On the termite construction site, there is no one in charge of the master plan, as such. Rather, each termite carries out a relatively simple task. They interact with each other and with the world around them through their senses of touch and smell. From these local inter-actions among thousands of termites, just as the case of the birds in the 'V' formation, impressive structures emerge.

Reason one for organizations refusing to evolve: Human beings have an innate 'centralized mindset', whereby we mistakenly assume that predictable results are possible only if there is someone to control the attempts to achieve them.

Leaders and powerful people in all times have been good at manipulating this inherent thinking in human beings, which Resnick refers to as the 'centralized mindset', instigating us to search for a central controlling point, be it in the universe, nation state or corporation. 'In fact, one of the main business techniques of control is to "engineer consent" so that the "intelligent minority" can rule,' says Chomsky. 'This intelligent and powerful minority, through several means, reiterate the fact that the general masses are nothing but a bewildered herd, too ignorant and incompetent to make sound decisions for themselves, and hence must be guided and governed by a few responsible men, the expert elites.'

Management thinkers Gary Gemmill and Judith Oakley (1992) might completely agree with Chomsky on this. They argued that this 'centralized mindset' in us is well exploited by the leaders, almost as if it is their secret agenda. They contend that the very notion of leadership is 'an alienating social myth' to encourage passivity in followers, so that they remain comfortable in their lowly roles, resigned to the fact that, after all, higher-order changes can be brought about only by the actions of distinguished individuals. This maintenance of the status quo, where only certain members of a social system are at the apex of power, sows seeds of helplessness, mindlessness, emotionlessness and meaninglessness in subordinates, resulting in a massive intellectual and emotional deskilling on a societal scale. The social myth around leaders serves to programme life out of people who, with this social lobotomization, appear as cheerful robots. Warren Bennis, widely regarded as the pioneer in leadership studies, asserts the same point – that leadership is ultimately an unconscious conspiracy, or social hoax, aimed at maintaining the status quo.

Reason two for organizations refusing to evolve: People in leadership positions exploit their followers by keeping them suppressed in their lowly roles. They actively sow seeds of helplessness and mindlessness in their lives.

However, even if one accepts that our theory of centralized mindset is correct, we still are left with a bigger question to answer. Why have corporations or organizations stood the test of time, even as nation states – the higher order economic entities – and families – the building blocks of the society – have evolved into forms that are more democratic?

Chomsky says that corporations are still standing as totalitarian institutions because they are primarily a product of the Anglo-American societies, where they dominate not only the business sphere but also the political life, media and basic intellectual culture. Corporate power has evolved as the epicentre of these cultures, such that they exert a significant control over the media, press agents and other means of publicity and propaganda, and hence a control over the mode of communication in society. Chomsky quotes John Dewey, an influential American philosopher, who wrote that as long as the private powers have control over the means of exchange of information, none of the popular movements or popular organizations would rise above the existing structures of power.

Chomsky has a case to demonstrate his point – that of US Steel, which about 30 years back decided to close a major plant in the steel town of Youngstown, Ohio, where the core of the community had been built up around it. The workers and the community came out in the streets in protest. They argued that instead of the company closing down the plant, they should be allowed to take it over and run it and earn the profit for their own benefit. They brought a case up through the courts, arguing that the management rules ought to be changed so that stakeholders, rather than just shareholders, would have control over the corporation. It was a perfectly feasible idea, but still lost in the courts, as the authorities of US Steel chose to lose money rather than give it away to the workers. 'It is not surprising that no one knows about it because it was never reported in the media. Media houses are also ultimately corporations and they do not want to publicize this kind of a thing,' laments Chomsky.

Reason three for organizations refusing to evolve: Organizations dominate not only business but also other social spheres, controlling the vital communication links in society.

Gemmil and Oakley support this view of Chomsky's, as they argue that the major significance of most studies on leadership is not to be found in their scientific validity but in their function of offering ideological support for the existing social order – where leaders rule and subordinates are ruled. Books on organizational psychology, management and particularly popular literature continue to reiterate our belief in the disproportionate influence of a single leader on our organizations. The 'Father of Management', Frederick W Taylor, is definitely one such person to be blamed; more than a century ago, he helped to firmly establish a rigid hierarchy with his theory of 'brains at the top', 'hands at the bottom' – popularized through his writings. Under Taylorism, actual thinking or initiative on the part of 'the hands' was actively discouraged, as it would potentially undermine the leadership of 'the brains'.

Reason four for organizations refusing to evolve: Popular magazines and media reiterate the Taylorian myth of 'brains at the top', 'hands at the bottom'.

However, the media are not the only ones to be blamed for the continuing totalitarianism in organizations. In fact, there is another surprising culprit – the existing democratic political states and their governments. Initially, the monarchs held their fortress of authority by plundering and amassing a state's wealth for themselves, mostly in the form of land. However, the rise of the money economy changed these equations, as wealth passed to the entrepreneurial class. They rose to such prominence that even rulers required their economic might to shield their throne and authority. 'The Anglo-American corporations continue to be the bulwark of their national governments, while the rulers reciprocate by safeguarding these corporate interests,' comments Chomsky.

John Dewey rightly concluded that: 'Politics is the shadow cast on society by big businesses,' as Chomsky comments, because ours is ultimately a business-run society:

> In fact, business corporations of today run a virtual senate, who carry out a moment-by-moment referendum on government policies. If they find that any of these policies are against them, meaning they help people instead of profits, they vote against by capital flight, tax on the country and so on. So, the democratic states of today have a dual constituency, their own population and the virtual senate, who often prevail.

Chomsky concludes:

> Though it threatens and undermines the fundamental principal of equality in a democratic society, corporations, by exerting their influence on their governments, have made sure that they are granted the equal rights and privileges of a citizen, in the process creating a unique class of people with unprecedented access to financial resources, limited legal accountability and virtual immortality. Moreover, unlike real individuals, who function with the guidance of complex moral guidelines, possess sensitivity to social norms, and who presumably seek to co-exist peacefully with their neighbours, corporations exist solely to consolidate wealth and accumulate power. They are completely unaccountable and are not responsible to anybody other than their own profits. In allowing the government system to aid corporations in accumulating profit, the state essentially has agreed to use its own resources (ie of the people) to support corporations' efforts to accumulate more wealth into the hands of fewer people.

Reason five for organizations refusing to evolve: Even democratic governments of our time need the economic might of organizations to shield their power and authority. Hence, they protect them.

Dr John Maxwell, celebrated leadership author, who strives towards building more leaders across the world, offers yet another reason why organizations are not yet evolving. He suggests that different institutions and different communities need not evolve at the same pace, and concludes:

> When a transition happens, it does not simultaneously happen in all groups. A few groups will break out and would make that transition happen. When that transition is successful, it starts spreading to the other groups. Businesses have been slow because of a couple of reasons. One, because money is involved. Whenever money is involved, power is involved. People who have the money are least likely to want to open that up and share that. In businesses, one who has the golden goose sets golden rules. But eventually, the power equations here again will change. For sure (2010).

Reason six for organizations refusing to evolve: Organizations, unfortunately, have been laggards in democratic evolution.

Why the time has come for organizations to transform into democracies

Many theories of political philosophy, sociology and organizational behaviour find parallels between the development of families, organizations and nation states. In fact, some of them even suggest that they are nothing but mirror images of each other. However, though families and nation states evolved into more digestible democratic forms from their initial totalitarian states of existence, organizations still seem to be stuck. The media, through their publicity and propaganda about the disproportionate influence of a single leader on our organizations, have definitely played a large role in maintaining the status quo in our organizations.

'But this is changing,' says Alex Haslam, Professor of Social and Organizational Psychology at the University of Exeter. Popular literature and books on leadership initially harped on a 'great man idea', which was about an extraordinary figure qualified to lead by virtue of some special quality that set him (or her) apart from other people. These qualities were supposed to be evidence of the leader's superior fitness. They cannot be learned and cannot be imitated, and hence these people were special and deserved special recognition and rewards. Thus, these people were thought to be at the core of history and progress. But as Alex Haslam observes:

several problems with this great man idea started showing up, especially when people started becoming increasingly interested in their lives, their unique qualities and psychology. When academics and theoreticians started looking at the distinguishing attributes of these great people, they found it increasingly difficult to testify in any meaningful way. Effectively, they could not come up with any convincing answers about any extraordinary powers which these leaders possessed compared to others.

Slowly, there started a shift in focus, where organizational theorists increasingly came to the conclusion that the people they studied were not great leaders because of any special qualities that they possessed, but because of the greatness of the groups that they led. It effectively became not an individual trait, but a group trait. So the core purpose of the great man approach now changed, to throw the analytical spotlight on the role of the group in promoting that leader's success, and the role of the individual leader in facilitating and allowing the group to achieve the goals that they have set out to achieve. This perspective forced us to see leadership not as a process that revolved around individuals acting and thinking in isolation, but as a group process in which leaders and people are joined together in a shared endeavour (Haslam, Reicher and Platow, 2010).

Reason one why this is the right time for organizational evolution: In academic circles and popular literature, the 'great man idea' of leadership is giving way to 'group leadership'.

Dr John Maxwell thinks that this shift of focus – from one great man to the shared efforts – by academies, popular literature and media in hastening the evolution of totalitarian organizational environments into more democratic ones.

> In America in the 1980s, if you went to the book store, and if you wanted a business book, you would have picked up a management book, which delved into how to manage people in an organizational context. In the '90s that started changing. The management books started going off the shelf. And they started being replaced with leadership books. The pace of life started to move very fast.

Until then, the assumption was that everything stays the same. However, as the environment around started moving at a fast pace, people had to catch up with it. That meant they had to lead. The '90s was almost the edge of the leadership book movement. Therefore, leadership became a major subject of learning throughout the world. However, when we came into this decade we have another transition happening in the case of popular books' focus. We are going from one-man-centric leadership books to a team of leaders taking charge. So, it is no longer one person in charge, but a group of people in charge.

That was a natural transition, because culture today is a changed one. Things have become so complicated that one person is not able to lead alone. Things have also changed in such a way that people are now less willing to take any one person's direction. They want to be equally involved in decision making. They expect dialogues and feedback. Organizational change is faster now than ever before.

Reason two why this is the right time for organizational evolution: The fast-changing environment is forcing people to look beyond one leader for solutions.

Dr Maxwell says that organizations of today are forced to look beyond their totalitarian culture more now than ever before. The media are playing a role but, more importantly, a self-realization is growing, among both the leaders and their people, that it takes more than just one leader to handle the increasingly complicated environment. Until recently, people had thrived on the assumption that one person had answers to all the questions. That worked in the past. But today suddenly they have to cope with stranger realities. As Dr Maxwell remarks:

> In so many years of my interaction with organizations, I am yet to come across a leader who has the capability to lead in every situation, every time and in every area. Leaders who realize this sufficiently early search for others within their organizations who can complete and complement them. Complement them in such a way that they can put their heads together to generate more ideas. More ideas that could help them compete better in today's most competitive market place. Because great ideas come from interactions. They come from sharing, and not from keeping to oneself.

Dr Ram Raghavan, a UK-based consultant who has been studying the human brain for the last couple of decades to develop and customize models to profile people, performance and processes in organizations, reiterates the importance of looking beyond one leader in an organization for all the answers. He has a unique reasoning about this. He says, considering the fact that the human brain operates at a miniscule 100 Hertz compared with the gigahertz or terrahertz super-computers of today, it has to screen and process information in the smartest way possible. Hence, although there are designated areas in the brain for certain functions, it also has to draw from and link multiple areas while performing complex tasks. So even when identical twins experience a specific event, the neural currents generate different imprints and different patterns – enabling different people to have different interpretations of the same event, or enabling them to notice different nuances of it. When handling a complicated situation, two brains are always better than one. And five are definitely better than just two.

'It is rather simple. As my friend, Ken Blanchard says "one of us is not as smart as all of us". Organizational leaders who follow this have made themselves ready for today's marketplace. Else, they would be soon in for a surprise,' suggests Dr Maxwell:

> After organizational leaders read my *21 Irrefutable Laws of Leadership*, they started coming back to me and saying that though they are good in, say, six laws, they are below average in the rest of them. At the same time, all these laws were important, that none of them could be ignored. So, the bigger question was how to make sure that, organizationally, they have all these laws in place. We came over to the same answer – do not depend on one leader. Develop a leadership team around you, where leaders can complement others, as well as develop their people, that they can all contribute to the organizational progress.

Dr Maxwell continues:

> Let me draw a good example from my life. When I was shifting my company from one location to another, I could have continued to lead the team. No one would have questioned my leadership. Yet, I chose Frank. Because I knew, Frank was excellent when it came to attention to detail, which I lacked. I was aware that I was not a person who could do daily follow-ups that a transition project required. I handed over the charge completely to Frank. For the next 12 months, he chartered the course for our venture. During this time, I followed him. So, in today's changing world, leaders should understand not only their strengths, but also their weaknesses. They should also understand the strengths and weaknesses of their fellow leaders. Therefore, leaders lead and leaders also follow. Followers follow and they also lead sometimes.

Reason three why this is the right time for organizational evolution: Leaders are increasingly becoming aware that they are not equipped to do everything alone.

Why organizations have no option but adopt democracy, if they want to survive

So, the media are opening our organizational leaders' thinking towards democratic possibilities in their workplaces. The changed realities of today are forcing them to adopt what they are reading and hearing. However, there is another powerful reason for organizations to change to forms that are more democratic – evolution. Organizations not only should be and could be democratic; they may also have to be – whether some of them like it or not. For example, nation states and families advanced towards democracy not because it was politically correct, but because it was the only system that could withstand the onslaught of evolution. In short, democracy arrived because it offered evolutionary stability, a state where competing forces in a system are balanced, in such a way that they need not change any further to accommodate transformations in the external and internal environments. The crumbling of many of the existing autocratic regimes that we are witnessing, across realms, is again not accidental. Anything that did not have the evolutionary stability just had to give in and perish.

Democracy is such a state of evolutionary stability for socio-economic systems like nation states, families and organizations. As they get older (which could take centuries or even millennia), they move away from totalitarian models – characterized by class struggles, conflicts of interests and inequalities – towards democracies – marked by a better balance of power, optimization of rewards for groups and minimization of overall costs. Yes, even in this state, there are compromises between groups and group members, but overall the system is in a well-oiled machinery mode, almost future-ready, as it moves into a state of democracy.

Organizations will evolve towards democracy because it is the only evolutionarily stable form.

Christian List of the London School of Economics, and Larissa Conradt of the University of Sussex, in England, who study group decision making in humans and animals, offer us substantial evidence to the fact that democracy is evolutionarily more stable for groups than the other forms. One of the important reasons that they give is the cost involved in making decisions in a group. They write that, quite contrary to our conventional thinking, under most conditions the costs to the subordinate group members, and to the group as a whole, are considerably higher for totalitarian than for democratic groups. They write (2009):

> Every individual knowingly or unknowingly incurs a cost as a decision is made in a group that he is a part of. This cost to individual group members depends on their own ability to influence the outcome versus that of other group members. For example, when CEOs dictate corporate decisions, this will incur only minimum cost to them because they would choose outcomes that are optimal for themselves or their shareholders. However, the subordinate members will incur higher costs according to how different their own optima are from those of the CEO. By contrast, if the group could agree on a decision outcome that is preferred by a majority of members, then the costs would

be relatively lower for most members in the group. While the autocrat alone benefits and pays lower costs in a totalitarian group, all other members benefit from a democratic decision.

At the same time, this does not mean that the totalitarian CEO does not incur any cost at all, even though the decisions are optimal for him/herself. As subordinates agree to fall in line with their CEO's decisions, they are in fact decreasing their individual influence, and are giving up on their individual choices and preferences. People usually do not want to do that or might not automatically do that. This means that the autocrat also incurs a cost – a cost of enforcing a despotic decision, typically done in our organizations through means such as coercion, manipulation or incentivization. So democracy is not only beneficial for most members in terms of lower costs, it might also bring down a part of the CEO's costs, making it a better long-term proposition than totalitarianism.

Reason one for the evolutionary advantage of democracy: Democracy considerably lowers the cost for the majority of individual members in the organization.

The evolutionary advantage of the democratic model does not end with lower individual costs. Totalitarian decisions, even when the leader happens to be the most experienced group member, would incline towards one extreme, because they are taken by one or a few individuals, representing only their vested interests. This extremity in decision making can easily lead to disaster, since a single person would never be able to consider all possibilities and probabilities. In democratic decision making, every individual has a stake, and hence would be able to add his or her perspective to it, making the ultimate decision less extreme and hence more realistic. Democracy engages public expectations, opinions and preferences within a framework of checks and balances that, according to US political scientist Samuel Huntington, result in better predictability of events. Without such checks and balances, shocks to the system would have a greater and wider social impact. Democratic structures that regulate totalitarian decisions help the overall system to be more resilient and adaptable to the complex and varying environment of today.

The 'Jury Theorem' proposed by the 18th-century French philosopher Nicolas de Condorcet points in the same direction: that contrary to our conventional thinking, decisions made by large groups of people are more likely to turn out to be accurate than decisions made by individuals. Even if each member of a jury has only partial information, the majority decision is more likely to be correct than a decision arrived by an individual juror. Additionally, the probability of a correct decision increases with the size of the jury. Condorcet's theory underlines the evolutionary stability of democratic structures, since they tend to outperform autocratic ones.

Reason two for the evolutionary advantage of democracy: Democratic decisions tend to be less extreme and hence bring in more predictability of results.

Democracy also has an overall impact on the morale of group members. In a totalitarian set-up, since decisions are imposed on them, people would seldom invest their full potential in carrying them out. Eventually, the group as a whole would lose out, as their performance would be less than optimal at all times. In the longer term, this could mean lower group morale, reduced innovative spirits and lowered competitive advantage. Dr Ram Raghavan narrates an example drawn from the military, where generals, who are essentially like CEOs, devise strategies and communicate them downwards for conversion into tactics and results. Subordinates obey their general and follow orders to implement the strategy devised. Yet many strategies fail on the ground, often because subordinates are not truly convinced about the suitability of the strategy, and sometimes do not even believe in the end objectives. As subordinates, they accept the orders and implement them, but as real people, they are not convinced, which leads to failure. Soldiers who have little or no trust in their superiors do not fight to 'win', they fight to 'survive' for another day. Lasting success can only be ensured when generals as well as subordinates are thinking alike.

Reason three for the evolutionary advantage of democracy: Democracy increases the stakes of individual members in the system and hence has a positive effect on their overall morale and ultimate results.

The bandits of yesterday realized that they gained more by settling down in one village than constantly roaming around. However, as they settled, the villagers found that was to their advantage also, since it offered them physical security from other barbarians. It was better to be looted by one than several. As time passed, what started out as a totalitarian rule gave in to the desires of the ruled. The volatile totalitarian system moved closer towards democracy and evolutionary stability – in nation states as well as in families. Organizations, though currently lagging behind, will ultimately have to take the same route. They have to settle down in an evolutionary equilibrium offered by democracy. The sooner they do that, the better.

References

Acemoglu, D and Robinson, J (2006) *Economic Origins of Dictatorship and Democracy*, Cambridge University Press, New York

Bhargava, S (2010) Personal interview, 15 March

Chomsky, N (2010) Personal interview, 3 June

Conradt, L, Krause, J, Couzin, ID and Roper, TJ (2009) 'Leading according to need' in self-organizing groups, *American Naturalist*, 173 (3) [Online] www.princeton.edu/~icouzin/Conradtetal2009.pdf (accessed 3 March 2009)

Conradt, L and List, C (2009) Group decisions in humans and animals: a survey, *Philosophical Transactions of the Royal Society of London*, Series B, Biological sciences, 364 (1518), pp 719–42

Conradt, L and Roper, TJ (2003) Group Decision-Making in Animals, *Nature*, 421 (January), pp 155–58

Dunlap, A (1996) *Mean Business: How I save bad companies and make good companies great*, Touchstone, 1996

Durant, W (1993) *The Story of Civilization*, Mjf Books, republished in June 1993

Gemmill, G and Oakley, J (1992) Leadership: an alienating social myth? *Human Relations*, 45 (2), pp 113–29

Haslam, A, Reicher, S and Platow, M (2010) *The New Psychology of Leadership, Identity, Influence and Power*, Psychology Press, London

Malone, T (2004) *The Future of Work*, Harvard Business School Press, Boston

Maxwell, J (2010) Personal interview, 19 March

Menon, Vijaya (2010) Personal interview, 2 March

Mynampati, R (2009) Interview in *The Times of India*, 8 January

Olson, M (2000) *Power and Prosperity*, Basic Books, New York

Resnick, M (1996) Beyond the centralized mindset, *Journal of the Learning Sciences*, 5 (1), pp 1–22

Stein, H (2007) Organizational totalitarianism and the voices of dissent, *Journal of Organizational Psychodynamics*, 1 (Spring)

Viswanathan, J (2006) *Social Origins of Democracy'*, MSS Research paper

Leadership
Making waves

03

ELENA P ANTONACOPOULOU

Acknowledgements

In developing these ideas I had the benefit of testing them in conversation with a range of practitioners (scholars and executives) who have provided me with much valuable feedback as well as inspiration. In some cases they also introduced me to relevant sources that are cited in this chapter and that informed some of my thinking. I thank each of them in no particular order for the difference they made to my thinking: Regina Bento, Larry Prusak, Kristian Mjoen, Paul Oliver, Helen Smith, Terry Parry.

Introduction

As the idea of leadership continues to grow in research and business practice over time, it appears that we are reaching a moment in its history where leadership is in danger of meaning everything and nothing. On the one hand, it may be argued that this is typical of the way management ideas develop, especially when we have come to see them as integral to all aspects of life and not just life in work organizations alone. On the other hand, however, this fuzziness around the meanings of leadership makes it all the more urgent to take active steps to rescue the idea so that a clear set of meanings can be distilled to inspire and inform future research and business practice.

This chapter is a direct response to this need. Building on my previous analyses, which have problematized the mystique underlying the way leadership is frequently presented in everyday discourse, in this chapter I present a fresh deconstruction of the word leadership by coining the term 'leader-ship'. In doing so, the aim is to draw attention to two fundamental issues that merit particular attention in the way the idea of leadership is developed and enacted in future research and business practice.

The two aspects are: the *leader* as a version of 'man' – homo – which is examined here focusing on phronesis.[1] Expanding on earlier discussions of leadership in relation to phronesis, this chapter will present the leader through the perspective of homo-phroneticus. This will explicate why leaders may qualify to be recognized as such, by paying attention not only to their practices but also the intentions, choices, practical judgements and actions that constitute such practices. This perspective extends the practice view of leadership developed elsewhere (see Antonacopoulou and Bento, 2010) and draws particular attention to the qualities of homo-phroneticus that would be distinct from versions of leadership founded on other dominant versions of man, such as homo-economicus and homo-sociologicus.[2]

The second important aspect of this re-conceptualization of leader-ship is the *ship*. The analysis of what constitutes the ship in leadership provides both a literal and metaphorical way of accounting for personal impact, a topic that has not received sufficient attention in leadership studies thus far. This chapter will explicate impact and what it would mean in leadership and will do so by drawing on references of impact as a process of making waves (Antonacopoulou, 2009, 2010a). The discussion will also provide a basis for articulating personal impact akin to a process of making waves that can have consequences well beyond what leaders may have anticipated in the intentions, choices and actions they have taken.

This point draws attention to the power of leadership to move. This latter point is explicated through references to examples that form part of a global programme of research that seeks to capture examples of leader-ship among ordinary people. The essential point that this analysis instrumentally makes, is that the power of leader-ship lies among ordinary people who can demon-strate extra-ordinary leadership. Such leadership is powerful, because it moves. It mobilizes action, not just that of the leader but that of others who form part of the perturbations of the wave and movement that is part of what makes leadership distributed and shared. This point draws attention to the extra-ordinary consequences of leadership that like waves energize and extend the scope for making a difference through actions that have the potential to transform the impossible into the possible.

These ideas are discussed in this chapter in the order outlined above and provide the foundation for some emerging questions that are offered by way of an invitation to action rather than a set of conclusions. By ending this chapter with an invitation, we signal that the idea of leader-ship hopefully marks the beginning of a new journey in which I invite others to join on a global scale.

The *leader* in leadership: man as *homo-phoneticus*

Leadership as an idea in everyday discourse describes those – so called 'leaders' – who are often presented as being extraordinary, demonstrating qualities that are unique, akin to super-humans. The legendary image through which leaders are being presented positions them in a league of their own. Leaders are heroes and, in the management and organization studies literature in particular, their unique status in history is earned by their success – most frequently their success in delivering financial prosperity to businesses. Therefore, it is not uncommon for leadership to be associated with winning and celebrating achievements of extraordinary proportions. Ironically, reaching the pinnacle of success is often presented with little account for any struggle, pain and suffering. It almost seems that leaders emerge to their status miraculously as if they were meant to be that way. This adds to the mystique that leadership entails, which makes narratives of leaders create on the one hand a promising world of possibility that everyone could envision, and on the other hand a promising world of possibility that very few can be part of and only a handful can deliver.

The debate on leadership has come a long way in accounting for the vulnerability implicit in not knowing, the need for openness to engage with the insecurity of the unknown rather than clinging to the comforting security of false competence. Like others I have maintained a particular interest in the way leadership may be learned; and in advancing ideas in relation to *learning leadership* (see Antonacopoulou and Bento, 2003, 2010), I have also been particularly interested in explicating how leadership practice is practised (Antonacopoulou, 2008).

Practising: becoming a leader

Practising reflects a process of becoming that is tentative and ongoing. It is not merely a process punctuated by events or activities, it is a movement that develops and unfolds through the intensity of connections that drive the process of becoming. This means that practising entails rehearsing, refining, learning, unlearning and changing actions and the relationships between different elements of an action (intension, ethos, internal and external goods, phronesis etc). Practising is as much a process of repetition as it is a space, embracing the multiplicity of possibilities as different (new) dimensions are (re)discovered in a moving horizon where past, present and future meet. Practising is the *deliberate, habitual and spontaneous repetition* reflective of the dynamic and emergent nature of action (see Antonacopoulou, 2004, 2006). I have also been instrumental in highlighting that practising has repetition at its core, and that repetition in the context of practising is not a mechanistic process of replication. *Replication* implies institutionalization in the process of re-presentation and re-production. *Repetition* on the other hand, implies transgression, perfection and integration (Deleuze, 1994). Repetition forms a condition of movement, a means of producing something new in history.

Practising applied to leaders and leadership reveals the importance of experiencing a crisis in learning, akin to how unlearning may be understood, where discovering different ways of embodying leadership are possible through engagement with the process of leading. Practising also entails visualization and immense concentration in rehearsing again and again aspects of leadership differently, but without necessarily referring to such acts as leadership per se. This implies that while practising one is also improvising, and hence loosening the structure once in the act. This means that the practice of leading becomes second nature for the leader to the extent that they *are* their leadership. Practising leadership, therefore, is about learning leadership that is founded not on the promise of success but on the promise of engaged participation. Such a process of practising leadership is akin to a search for perfection where failure and disappointment are integral to the pursuit of leadership not as a goal but as a possibility.

This draws attention to leadership practice, reflecting beyond its social character a very personal commitment that requires complete devotion, persistence and perseverance, courage and idealism. These qualities reveal that leadership is not only about purposeful action. Leadership is also about forging powerful connections through actions that transform the impossible into the possible. This is what makes leadership an engaged act. Engagement, etymologically, is as much about commitment and connectivity as it is about something being under pledge. Engaging in leadership is therefore a promise and a vow to pursue a recognized need honourably, which goes beyond simply achieving desirable results. This point draws an important distinction between process (pursuing a goal) and outcome (achieving a result). The former draws more attention to the ongoing effort, the making and doing that any action entails. The latter draws attention to the result and mostly to positive results – success. The process of pursuing a goal involves persistently and systematically trying things out – simply put, *practising*.

Practising then reveals the embodied nature of action. The actions of leaders are not only a matter of choice and the responsibility and accountability entailed. Action is also a reflection of what leaders care about, what they may have a passion for. Beyond desire and passion, action also entails the very personal commitment to what becomes a chosen goal. This personal commitment forms the orientation of leadership in relation to the human power of leaders who strive for excellence, growing through their leadership as people and discovering their humanity.

The choices leaders make are a reflection both of their identity and self-image, and of their motivations and virtues. They are what Carlsen (2006) calls 'life enrichments' in the search for higher purpose and in the process of improvisation and imagination. To understand practising leadership is not simply a case of seeking meaningfulness in human behaviour (see Harré and Secord, 1972). For, if we only focus on the observable behaviours, we will fail to see what lies beneath and what the essence of leadership is: *phronesis* (practical judgment).

The leader as homo-phroneticus

The Aristotelian notion of *phronesis* (see Aristotle, *Nicomachean Ethics*, and interpretations by Dunne, 1993; Wall, 2003; Nonaka and Toyama, 2007; Eikeland, 2009) as a virtue attests to the power of practical judgment in agency. Phronesis provides access to the ways leaders negotiate competing priorities. It exposes the internal conflict they may often encounter and the ways such tensions form the basis of their power to excel in what they do by virtue of being who they are – individual – different. Phronesis is a means of making a difference through choices that reflect leadership at different points in time. Phronesis extends the standards of performance by providing space for judgments to be formed and choices to be made in how rules are applied and not just passively followed. In this sense, phronesis guides leaders who embody leadership in their conduct. It defines purposeful action by sensitizing leaders to be more aware of their intentions and the processes of trying, deciding, believing that an intention exists and will be pursued. Intentionality, therefore, is not only praxis and telos; it is also phronesis as it reflects virtues like justice, trustworthiness, courage and honesty (McIntyre, 1985). This means that at the core of phronesis is not just the knowledge that guides the actions taken, but also the everyday experiences where action is taken and decisions about action are made, all of which combine to form the character of the human. Hence, phronesis is a way of acting, thinking, knowing and living which is why it reflects the character of man described as *phronimos* (Noel, 1999).

The case for homo-phroneticus

This brief overview of phronesis (for more detailed analysis see Anton-acopoulou, 2010b, 2011) acts here to provide a foundation for explicating further the leader – man (irrespective of gender) – that lies in leader-ship. The discussion will advance the idea and ideal of what will be referred to as *homo-phroneticus*. The intention behind this analysis is to provide both a more rigorous analysis of the relationship between leadership and phronesis than those more recently postulated in the literature (see Nonaka and Takeuchi, 2011; McKenna, Rooney and Boal, 2009; Küpers and Statler, 2008) and in doing so, to provide a foundation for further exploration into the making of a leader and leadership in action.

My starting point is to draw on Van Manen's (1991) assertion that man experiences the world tactfully. He describes 'tact' as mindful action – a form of human interaction that implicates the 'immediacy of the actor in a situation, emotionally, responsively and mindfully'. This fundamentally reflects the concept that human actions in everyday life are reflections and expressions of who one is as a whole person. In this respect, situational action is linked 'to its sense rather than behaviour to its determinants', as Geertz (1983) asserts, because at root 'man is an animal suspended in webs of significance he himself has spun'. This point explicates the importance of recognizing why the actions we take and the process of making choices about such actions have implications well beyond the end to which they are directed. Hence, a phronetic perspective to our interpretation of human action places more emphatically the onus on action as an expression and reflection of who one is. Put differently, a phronetic orientation is a way of being that arises from one's self as a whole person. In other words, *homo-phroneticus* is as much about the practical judgements and difficult choices man makes in everyday life, fundamentally because such choices are a reflection of who man is, not only how man chooses between right or wrong but how man chooses to go about everyday life.

The key point in this analysis is the attention it draws to the intimate engagement of the actors in their acts of thinking, judging, knowing, acting and living. This *re-cognition* reveals the importance of *perception, critique* (*krisis*) and *imagination* (*phantasia*) as critical aspects of man's – leader's – actions. The essence here is the way man grasps a situation and chooses a course of action. This process of grasping a situation is as much founded on deliberation and dwelling as it is supported by sensation – *aesthesis* – which guides how man exercises choice by perceiving both the quiddity (the essence) and quality of an object or subject in a given situation by orchestrating the senses. Hence, instances of intuiting, imagining, harmonizing reflect the critical connection between emotions and cognitions invoked by the senses, which signals that man attends to situations with *synaesthesia* – not just by drawing on all the senses, but also with consciousness (which is also what the word *synaesthisis* means in Greek).

Conscience does not only point to the way good and bad, true and false are defined in different situations. It also signals that such categories are not only defined by situations, or indeed the social conditions that may guide choices and judgements. More fundamentally, it reveals man's capacity to imagine. Phantasia is in phronesis a drive that underpins why man may chose to seek or avoid a situation or an object or indeed a subject, depending on whether that which is brought to focus is perceived as relevant to man's concerns and interests. This point finds support in Dunne (1993) in relation to the centrality of phronesis as a continuation of the dynamism of experience, because it allows 'the greatest degree of flexibility, openness, and improvisation'. Wall (2003) takes this point further by reminding us that phronesis is 'poetic', because it implies at the very core the endless re-creation of social relationships and, I would add, images and possibilities for objects and subjects to connect and re-connect through the choices that their inter-subjectivity forces them to experience and experiment with in-tension and extension. This point would also suggest that in phronesis the making of something (a choice) is a creative act (I make dinner, I make a point, I make time, I make love). Homo-phroneticus therefore, to borrow Wall's (2003) assertion, 'dares to create' not just by being creative, with the choices made exercising critique and imagination. Perhaps the promise of recognizing homo-phroneticus' approach to performing such creative acts lies in the way he expresses his humanity as a way of *living his practice* and in doing so inviting others also to participate in its creation and re-creation.

Effectively, the idea of homo-phroneticus offers the possibility of exploring the connections between practice and practitioner, act and actor, by applying not only tacit or explicit modes of knowing as a foundation for interpreting human behaviour. Instead, homo-phroneticus exposes the importance of *krisis* (reflexive critique in discerning ones' engagement in practice) and *phantasia* (a virtue of interpretive power and a means of grasping situations by feeling one's way around them), which give birth to ideas and allow possibilities to grow even if previously perceived as unimaginable. Homo-phroneticus provides a fresh basis for exploring not only how but also why the things that man does matters, for *krisis* and *phantasia* provide the capacity to engage fully (through orchestrating the senses) with the world perceptually. This means that man's perception is a particular perspective that both limits and at the same time frees the impact leaders make.

This point offers scope to explicate the value added contribution of advancing the idea of man, and leaders in particular, as homo-phroneticus. Previous conceptualizations of man as 'rational-economic man', 'complex man', 'social man' and 'self-actualizing man' (see Schein, 1965), along with other classifications, reveal different aspects of human nature, especially in relation to what motivates, what affects different responses to situations experienced and, generally, how man functions in different contexts. In similar vein, two versions of homo-sapiens seem to dominate our current understanding of human action and social order: 'homo economicus' and 'homo sociologicus'. Reckwitz (2002) captures succinctly the distinctions between these two models of human nature, explaining that:

> The model of the homo economicus explains action by having recourse to individual purposes, intentions and interests; social order is then a product of the combination of single interests. The model of the homo sociologicus explains action by pointing to collective norms and values, that is to rules which express a social 'ought'; social order is then guaranteed by a normative consensus.

In similar fashion, I would propose that the model of homo-phroneticus explains action by drawing attention to choice. Choice is where action originates from, Aristotle reminds us. Hence, choices reveal what is hidden in our intentions – our desires and the logic that guides our judgments. Choices reveal man's character in a particular situation in the way man engages in critique and imagination in expressing his humanity. This perhaps is what may distinguish man from just doing something as opposed to doing something with love and for the love of it. By orchestrating his senses and through that engaging in many of his acts with love, homo-phroneticus feels his way around a situation and performs his practice by living his practice. This is the ultimate way of expressing his love for what he does. Is not love the ultimate of feelings? But also is not doing something for the love of it the ultimate of all acts?

Some of the clues in recognizing homo-phroneticus may be found both in the way man acts and the way man speaks of his acts in relation, for example, to an object as something man loves or even adores: '*I love this painting,*' '*I adore good food,*' '*this piece of music fills me with joy*'. Equally man speaks of his relationship with others in terms of love or hate or even different shades of liking someone, shaping their relationships accordingly. Perhaps however, the main challenge homo-phroneticus faces is loving themselves. This is where homo-phroneticus becomes not just a material being but also a spirit. Vices such as *narcissism* (self-focus, self-importance), *hubris* (over-confidence, dogmatism), *hamartia* (inability to see the whole) and *anagnosis* (vacuum of ignorance) threaten man's phronesis and practice (Ford, 2006).

Understanding the leader in leader-ship through the lens of homo-phroneticus celebrates man's ongoing development. Becoming a leader is a potential that lies in every man irrespective of gender, education, social class and other variations. The scope of cultivating the leader in man lies in the recognition that man is an ongoing work-in-progress, an innovation that lies in the discovery of the character of man. This is why understanding the leader through the lens of homo-phroneticus helps us appreciate also that in our journey of becoming who we have the potential to become – leaders – our choices, character and actions will reveal to us the power of our capacity to love and experience the impact of such love. This perhaps is what leader-ship challenges us most to be confronted with. I turn to this issue next.

The *ship* in leadership: making waves

In everyday discourse a ship refers to a vessel that floats on water, although over time it has emerged as a term that describes other modes of travel too. Due to its historical uses a ship symbolizes travelling, exploring the unknown and discovering something new, notwithstanding of course that it is also associated with slavery, environmental pollution and piracy. The captain as a figurehead may be our more immediate attempt at linking ship and leadership. However, in this chapter an alternative focus is offered, drawing on Greek mythology. A ship named *Argo*, after the man who built it, Argus, played an important part in carrying the sailors named after it – Argonauts

– who sailed with Jason to Colchis in his quest to find the Golden Fleece. The importance of this myth is not the heroic achievements of Jason, to whom we would more naturally seek to attribute the relationship to leadership. Instead, the important relationship I want to draw attention to is that between *Argo*-the-ship, Argus-its-creator and the Argonauts-its-sailors. All are bound by the same ideal to travel.

The art of travel

Argus created the ship *Argo* for the purpose of making Jason's and his sailors' trip possible. *Argo*-the-ship gained character in the craftsmanship that Argus applied in designing and building it and the way the Argonauts used it to accomplish the mission of the trip. In the most simple terms, *Argo* was a product of Argus's practice, just as much as Argus expressed his ultimate potential in creating *Argo*. The intimate relationship between creator and product, subject and object, practitioner and practice referred to earlier, is not limited in this duality. It transcends in the way it engages others to participate in the co-creation. This is where the Argonauts come in. *Argo* came to symbolize their own dreams and aspirations. It provided an opportunity not only to share a common goal, that of supporting Jason in obtaining the Golden Fleece. It also provided a platform for them to become sailors who transformed the dream of travelling – exploration and discovery, embracing horizons and conquering places, accomplishing missions – into their reality.

Mythical as this analysis may seem, it reflects the reality we see when ordinary people like Argus create projects like *Argo* and inspire others to become part of their original dream and take it to unimaginable proportions. They draw our attention to the unsung heroes who are the everyday leaders that do not need a senior executive role or a position of power to do just what they do – being themselves, exercising their choices of doing what they do, and inspiring others to do their bit in what emerges as a journey without a pre-fixed destination. It is this notion of travelling that the ship in leader-ship celebrates when the leaders and their choices and actions create ships/platforms that allow them and others to travel far and discover new worlds.

The art of travel lies in the way existing resources are utilized, how capabilities are advanced in the process of learning to navigate our way around the vast sea of possibilities we are part of. This perhaps helps us realize that the way we choose to travel is a reflection of the ways we engage in the quest of making our lives (beyond the constrains of work, and the struggle for survival, as De Botton, 2003, proclaims) meaningful. It is that search for meaning that our life-project revolves around and it is in its pursuit that human flourishing is possible. In travelling there is anticipation just as much as there is surprise, and in Yann Martel's account of the *Life of Pi*, the protagonist in his book, the travelling, whether fictional or not, is as much about whether the events happened for real as about the curiosity of discovering the human spirit in the challenges experienced. In travelling therefore, we are exposed to tensions that swing us between the real and unreal, the expected and unexpected. It is in travelling that our horizons expand, and justifiably too why Cavafy invites us in his well-known poem *Ithaka* to wish that the journey is a long one.[3] The art of travel, however, is not just about the journey and the experiences it provides that allow man to grow. Returning to the relationship between Argus, *Argo* and the Argonauts, travelling is also a recognition of the waves one makes in the course of the journey one pursues. I turn to this point next.

Making waves: realizing personal impact

Many of my current efforts to speak of impact in management research have prompted me to do so by referring to waves and the notion of 'making waves' (Antonacopoulou, 2009, 2010a, 2010c; Antonacopoulou et al, 2011). I find waves fascinating not only because they comprise opposites like feed-forward–feed-backward or up and down movements in their rippling effects. What I also love about waves is their permanence in the way they feature as an essential aspect of experiencing vast or small volumes of water, and yet their variation in the way they form is almost independent of the water they rely on to exist. For example, we have come to acknowledge waves of different kind (eg tidal waves, freak waves, tsunamis) depending on their size, potency, intensity and the weather conditions that may cause them or the natural phenomena (eg earthquakes) that provoke them. Another fascinating feature of waves is that they are still at times unnoticeable yet also constantly changing the landscape they touch – their presence is noticeable in the marks they leave behind. What I recognize in waves as 'objects' is not just their materiality but the ongoing unfolding they represent in their movements. They are part of the sea and can hardly be noticed if one casts one's eyes to the horizon. And yet they have a presence of their own in the ways they form, which are not always determined by the sea but by the air bubbles that their movements form, as much as the elements surrounding them. Maybe they are called waves because of all these characteristics, and yet naming them waves provides explanations for something much more complex and rather incomprehensible: something that may in fact be an aspect of life more generally, which we would not directly associate them with – humans have been called waves too (Malone, 2011). And yet, what we have considered much less is the possibility also of humans *making waves*. The latter, for me at least, offers an exciting prospect in understanding our humanity, and realizing our personal impact in the choices and judgments we make and the actions we take. Associating leadership with realizing our personal impact reflects an initial attempt to explore this.

Many of our current attempts to account for individual contributions, certainly in the context of organizations, lie in the way performance is evaluated in the results delivered. Many business executives have arisen to the status of leader (eg Apple's Steve Jobs, GE's Jack Welsh) not least due to the results they have mobilized in company performance, especially during their time as CEO. Their leadership title was earned on the basis of the performance indicators (predominantly profitability) they were evaluated against. Through transformational change initiatives they have sought to inspire just as much as to enforce a collective mode of performing among the workforce, creating a new cultural norm and mobilizing desirable behaviours. Performance has been the driving force in controlling the way resources – including human capital – are to be managed to achieve the predefined strategic ends. This notion of performance, which is very dominant in many performance management systems, not only continues to fail to deliver the performance outcomes expected. It also encourages more of a performing act, where impression management is the dominant response in an attempt to play by the rules of the game. It is beyond the scope of this analysis to provide a critique of performance management systems. What suffices to say, however, is that performance as an indicator for individual contribution is ill suited in its design as it fails to capture the personal impact that individuals make in what they do, how they do what they do, and why they do what they do the way they do it.

This point prompts me to also suggest that performance can perhaps be conceptualized as an act of giving when the variety of aspects that constitute it are not delineated by just focusing on the observable and reportable results. Instead, performance is also a means of capturing aspects of the impact that what one does reflects. In other words, it is not a prescription for action but a force that energizes and can awaken others to release their own energy. Seen in these terms, if performance were to be seen as an account of the personal impact that an individual makes, then it would be usefully conceptualized – instead of a cause-and-effect relationship – as part of the fluctuating working net of events, of dense intermeshing relationships and incomplete connections; an indeterminate movement, a flow, an energy that energizes.

If we account for performance as an expression of personal impact in these terms, then we come to also recognize that existing measures of performance are ill suited, not least because they limit the scope for impact rather than celebrate impact. This realization presents a great opportunity to radically rethink the ways that performance and impact are both measured and realized. We cannot realistically expect that every intention to deliver impact will create the desired effects. We need to become more willing to embrace what Chia and Holt (2009) call 'performative extravaganza'. These variations in performance provide scope for self-expression that is different and has the potential to *make a difference* by adding richness to life (one's own and that of others). This is what we may consider performance to be – a process of making waves where the impact of such waves has the scope to shape landscapes.

Amplitudes, directions and breaking-points of waves are difficult, if not impossible, to predict; they evade our usual approaches of measurement (size, weight, surface-conditions, etc), which underlie mechanical attempts at fixing and controlling our environment. Waves thus combine qualities of matter with those of movement and flux, urging us to question the categories we construct in a futile attempt to capture something that is constantly emerging and remains always unfinished and open-ended. The wave is certainly there, it has substance and it is continually moving. The substance of the wave, however, is temporary, fluent and fragile, something that makes each wave a novelty of its own. It is fundamentally infused with difference and change, and the (dissipative) similarity with itself over time (making a movement in water seem like 'a' wave). For the spectator the (always fresh) image of 'a wave' is sufficiently precise as to give meaning, but not so mathematically precise as to display transcendent perfection. Making waves then would be considered a process of performing where the unfolding impact often becomes evident after long periods of concealed building up and changes in refraction and speed.

Making waves as an expression of the personal impact is also a creative act. It signifies homo-phroneticus – making waves – by expressing through his practice who he is, exploring in the process what he can become and doing so by living his practice through others who participate in it. In short, an ordinary man like Argus created *Argo*, which became a ship that the Argonauts used to navigate their way in search of their own Ithaka as much as Jason's quest for the Golden Fleece. In the bigger scheme of things, this myth does not only symbolize how man's creation (Argus building *Argo*) was an act of making waves that energized others (the Argonauts) to pursue their own journey. It continues to travel today as a story that, mythical or real, continues to move us in ways that depend on how we chose to engage with it. It is these stories of ordinary people demonstrating extraordinary leadership in making waves that the last section celebrates. These stories are intended as illustrative examples and invitations to reflect on what may otherwise go unnoticed in our everyday life unless some (ordinary people) do notice and chose to do something about it.

Extraordinary leadership by ordinary people

The story of Jorge Muñoz, a Columbian school bus driver from Queens New York, and that of Mukhtaran Bibi (otherwise known as Mukhtar Mai), a mature woman from the village of Meerwala in the Punjab area of Pakistan, are two examples extensively discussed elsewhere (see Antonacopoulou and Bento, 2010, and associated websites), reflecting ordinary people who demonstrated extraordinary leadership in response to a need they experienced at first hand and chose to do something about. In what they chose to do, Jorge Muñoz and Mukhtar Mai reflected their leader-ship. Their actions reinforce the principles of homo-phroneticus in the way we defined the leader aspect of leader-ship in the previous sections. They also provide an illustration of how each of these individuals and their actions created a 'ship' with multiple journeys. The ship in each case was something they made as a result of actions they took by exercising their choice to do something about a clear need they recognized.

In the case of Jorge Muñoz, that ship was a kitchen for cooking meals to feed hungry immigrants. For Mukhtar Mai, it was building a school to educate girls in a village where illiteracy allowed social norms to remove basic human dignity from women. But the ship was not just the set of actions they performed, nor the material objects that they created. Their impact was also the waves they made in building momentum, generating a movement that affected and infected others who chose to be involved and become part of the journey. The journey is what inspires participation, not just the destination. The ship provides the platform for many leaders to emerge and to participate. In the case of Jorge Muñoz, the Argonauts were his mother and sister, as well as over 100,000 viewers who have become dedicated fans and later sometimes sponsors of Muñoz's cause. Similarly, in Mukhtar Mai's case her Argonauts were her family, the police who protected her, the justice system that vindicated her and the girls in her school that learn with and from her, to name but a few. The impact of such leader-ship impacted also the leaders, 'ordinary' people who became world-recognized personalities. Jorge Muñoz was named a 'CNN Hero' and 'An Angel in Queens' for his charitable work in providing food for immigrants, while Mukhtaran Bibi was named as 'woman of the year' by *Glamour Magazine* and 'person of the week' by *ABC News*. She was renamed 'Mukhtar Mai' (meaning 'respected big sister') by the girls of the school she built next to her house with the financial award she received as compensation for being raped.

These illustrations of leader-ship that Jorge Muñoz and Mukhtar Mai reflect propelled a movement that has made waves strong enough to reach every part of the globe. This is leader-ship that is not limited by boundaries of geography, race, religion, gender or any other form of division that may be chosen as a barrier. Such leader-ship leaves no obstacle to restrict its path. It continues to travel and its destination emerges in the course of travelling with those that choose to become part of it. The essence of understanding leader-ship, therefore, lies in the way ordinary people demonstrate how extraordinary our humanity can be when it mobilizes us to act in ways that reveal our character.

Perhaps this offers a realization that the way we lead our lives is the ultimate call for the ship we create in our journey and, in doing so, the impact that we have on others intentionally and unintentionally. We can touch people by simply being who we are. There is a leader in us whose ship is ready to sail if only we have the courage to set it free. The human spirit, just as much as the human conscience and the human race, has travelled far over the centuries. Now perhaps is the moment to acknowledge that in celebrating our humanity we have scope to unleash even more amazing aspects of what being human means.

Invitation

It feels inappropriate to end this chapter with a set of conclusions. The motivation behind this chapter was to set the idea of leadership free. I hope instead to offer an invitation to the readers to take what they choose from this reconceptualization of leadership as *leader-ship*, and to do what their conscience calls them to do in their remit or work, life and world. I feel compelled as part of this invitation to pose three questions for consideration:

- When was the last time you stopped and had a good look around you and noticed things you were compelled to do something about?
- When was the last time someone reached out to recognize you for what you do and made you feel valued for being who you are (different)?
- Why wait to figure out the answer in both these questions and not act on both accounts now?

If you want to draw inspiration for acting in ways that make a difference, why not take a look at a true story... when in 1988, a teacher in New York acknowledged and honoured every one of her high school students. Then she invited her students to honour people throughout their community. One of these acknowledgments dramatically altered the life of a businessman and his 14 year-old son – **http://www.acknowledgmentmovie.com/**.

This story is one of many that illustrates how leader-ship makes waves. Leader-ship is a continuing odyssey. I wish you well in your travels. May the breeze of your conscience propel you in your journey. If you wish, please do share your story with others and with us in the global leader-ship programme (eagnosis@liv.ac.uk) that we are currently developing. If we are able to show how such leader-ship manifests itself in business organizations, then maybe we can make leadership mean so much more than our current conceptualizations limit it to. THANK YOU.

Notes

1 Phronesis is one of the types of knowledge Aristotle speaks about in *Nicomachean Ethics*. Phronesis or practical (praxis) knowledge (*Φρόνησις* – phronesis) is distinct from scientific (*Επιστήμη* – episteme) and technical (*Τέχνη* – techne) knowledge.

2 The terms 'homo' and 'man', along with the masculine pronoun, have been used in this chapter. This stems from a desire to avoid cumbersome language, and no discrimination, prejudice or bias is intended.

3 Ithaka

> As you set out for Ithaka
> hope the voyage is a long one,
> full of adventure, full of discovery.

Laistrygonians and Cyclops,
angry Poseidon – don't be afraid of them:
you'll never find things like that on your way
as long as you keep your thoughts raised high,
as long as a rare excitement
stirs your spirit and your body.
Laistrygonians and Cyclops
wild Poseidon – you won't encounter them
unless you bring them along inside your soul
unless your soul sets them up in front of you.

Hope the voyage is a long one.
There may be many a summer morning when,
with what pleasure, with what joy,
you come into harbors seen for the first time;
may you stop at Phoenician trading stations
to buy fine things,
mother of pearl and coral, amber and ebony,
sensual perfume of every kind –
as many sensual perfumes as you can;
and may you visit many Egyptian cities
to gather stores of knowledge from their scholars.

Keep Ithaka always in your mind.
Arriving there is what you are destined for.
But do not hurry the journey at all.
Better if it lasts for years,
so you are old by the time you reach the island,
wealthy with all you have gained on the way,
not expecting Ithaka to make you rich.

Ithaka gave you the marvelous journey.
Without her you would not have set out.
She has nothing left to give you now.

And if you find her poor, Ithaka won't have fooled you.
Wise as you will have become, so full of experience,
you will have understood by then what these Ithakas mean.

Translation by Edmund Keeley and Philip Sherrard – Princeton Paperbacks

References

Antonacopoulou, EP (2004) On the virtues of *practising* scholarship: a tribute to Chris Argyris a 'timeless learner', special issue, From Chris Argyris and Beyond in Organizational Learning Research, *Management Learning*, 35 (4), pp 381–95

Antonacopoulou, EP (2006) Working life learning: learning-in-practise, in *Learning, Working and Living: Mapping the terrain of working life learning*, ed

EP Antonacopoulou, P Jarvis, V Andersen, B Elkjaer, and S Hoeyrup, pp 234–54, Palgrave, London

Antonacopoulou, EP (2008) Practising engaged leadership: living the myth and embodying the legend of the Olympic athlete, in *Organizational Olympians*, ed M Kostera, pp 30–39, Palgrave, London

Antonacopoulou, EP (2009) Impact and scholarship: unlearning and practising to co-create actionable knowledge, *Management Learning*, 40 (4), pp 421–30

Antonacopoulou, EP (2010a) Making waves: moments when ideas are set free, in *Generativity in Qualitative Research*, ed A Carlsen and J Dutton, pp 158–61, CBS Press, Copenhagen

Antonacopoulou, EP (2010b) Making the business school more 'critical': reflexive critique based on phronesis as a foundation for impact, *British Journal of Management*, Special Issue, Making the Business School More 'Critical', 21, pp 6–25

Antonacopoulou, EP (2010c) Beyond co-production: practice-relevant scholarship as a foundation for delivering impact through powerful ideas, *Public Money and Management*, Special Issue, The Politics of Co-production Research, 30 (4), pp 219–25

Antonacopoulou, EP (2011) Why matter matters: warm dark matter and homo-phroneticus, Paper presented at the 3rd International Symposium on Process Organization Studies, Theme: *How Matter Matters: Objects, Artefacts and Materiality in Organization Studies*, June 2011, Corfu, Greece

Antonacopoulou, EP and Bento, R (2003) Methods of 'learning leadership': taught and experiential, in *Current Issues in Leadership and Management Development*, ed J Storey, pp 81–102, Blackwell, Oxford

Antonacopoulou, EP and Bento, R (2010) Learning leadership in practice, in *Leadership in Organizations: Current issues and key trends*, 2nd Edn, ed J Storey, pp 71–92 , Routledge, London

Antonacopoulou, EP, Dehlin, E and Zundel, M (2011) The challenge of delivering impact: making waves through the ODC scholarship, *Journal of Applied Behavioral Science*, Special Issue, Bridging the Scholar-Practitioner Divide, 47 (1), pp 33–52

Aristotle, *Nicomachean Ethics*, trans D Ross (1984), Oxford University Press, New York

Carlsen, A (2006) Organizational becoming as dialogic imagination of practice: the case of the indomitable Gauls, *Organization Science*, 17 (1), pp 132–49

Chia, R and Holt, R (2009) *Strategy without Design*, Cambridge University Press, Cambridge

De Botton, A (2003) *The Art of Travel*, Penguin Books, London

Deleuze, G (1994) *Difference and Repetition*, Continuum, London

Dunne, J (1993) *Back to the Rough Ground: Practical judgement and the lure of technique*, University of Notre Dame Press, Notre Dame

Eikeland, O (2009) *The Ways of Aristotle: Aristotelian phronesis, Aristotelian philosophy of dialogue and action research*, Peter Lang, Bern

Ford, R (2006) Why we fail: how hubris, hamartia, and anagnosis shape organizational behavior, *Human Research Development Quarterly*, 17 (4), pp 481–89

Geertz, C (1983) *The Interpretation of Cultures: Selected essays,* Basic Books, NU New York

Harré, R and Secord, P (1972) *The Explanation of Social Behaviour*, Blackwell, Oxford

Küpers, W and Statler, M (2008) Practically Wise leadership: towards an integral understanding, *Culture and Organization*, 14, pp 379–400

Malone, D (2011) *The Secret Life of Waves*, BBC4 documentary

Martel, Y (2003) *Life of Pi*, Cannongate Books, Edinburgh

McIntyre, A (1985) *After Virtue: A study in moral theory*, Duckworth, London

McKenna, B, Rooney, D and Boal, KB (2009) Wisdom principles as a meta-theoretical basis for evaluating leadership, *The Leadership Quarterly*, 20, pp 177–90

Noel, J (1999) On the varieties of phronesis, *Educational Philosophy and Theory*, 31 (3), pp 273–89

Nonaka, I and Takeuchi, H (2011) *The Wise Leader*, Harvard Business Review, May, pp 58–67

Nonaka, I and Toyama, R (2007) Strategic management as distributed practical wisdom (phronesis), *Industrial and Corporate Change*, 16 (3), pp 371–94

Reckwitz, A (2002) Toward a theory of social practices: a development in cultural theorizing, *European Journal of Social Theory*, 5 (2), pp 243–63

Schein, EH (1965) *Organizational Psychology*, Prentice-Hall, New York

Van Manen, M (1991) Reflectivity and the pedagogical moment: the normativity of pedagogical thinking and acting, *Journal of Curriculum Studies*, 23 (6), pp 507–36

Wall, J (2003) Phronesis, poetics and moral creativity, *Ethical Theory and Moral Practice*, 6, pp 317–41

'I'm not really a leader'
The power and impact of implicit leadership theories

TRACEY MANNING

04

It's absolutely predictable. In every leadership programme or graduate leadership class I conduct, at least one participant will confess: 'I'm not really a leader.' Others in the group will look surprised or nod supportively and (sometimes) admit the same about themselves. All this in programmes for managers – or aspiring leaders! You might guess that these were usually the younger participants or newer managers, but the response, and the belief, span participant ages and even levels of management.

I've even watched people who've been managers for a while and who have leadership roles in other areas of life (in religious congregations or other volunteer settings) vigorously defend their 'non-leadership' against those who challenge them. One manager, taxed by me and by her classmates with evidence of her work promotions, her church elder role and her volunteer leadership activities, still insisted she wasn't really a leader, she just 'did what was needed'.

What's going on here?

If they're not just being modest – and most aren't – people who claim they're not leaders find what they know about leaders inconsistent with what they know about themselves. They've compared themselves to their mental models of leaders and have concluded that they're not in that category. These mental categories integrating what we 'know' about leaders and leadership are called *implicit leadership theories*; they are culturally shared assumptions about how leaders develop, look and behave (Lord and Maher, 1993).

Most people know about racial and gender stereotypes, but may not realize that we humans use many types of mental categories, called schemas, as shortcuts to avoid extensive thinking. Schemas help our brains process a constant and potentially overwhelming amount of incoming information very quickly and efficiently. Without schemas to speed thinking and reacting, our lives would be chaotic or even paralysed! We would have to approach each new experience entirely fresh, gathering more information about it in a lengthy process before deciding how to think and act about it.

Schemas are dynamic; they are not passive categories into which we put information as into a file. They're more like software program, such as Adobe Acrobat or Microsoft Word, in that they 'grab' incoming information relevant to their specific focus. Closely associated with schemas are 'scripts', tendencies to respond emotionally and/or behaviourally to what we perceive. For instance, the sight of a uniformed police officer would probably trigger our schema for police, and an order from the police officer to move away from an accident site would likely trigger our script of obeying police officers. (Obviously not everyone has the same schema and script for police officers, but the police schema and script will be widely shared across a given culture.)

Schemas cover a wide range of groups and situations, everything from our individual identity to social norms, from what's edible to work roles, so that without thinking consciously we quickly size up most experiences and react accordingly. Discrete schemas are often organized into categories with multiple premises/beliefs, like the police example. We might have body types, personality characteristics, tendencies to behaviour, assumptions about corruptibility (or not), associated in our 'police' schema.

A stereotype is a type of schema, with the same function of speedy processing, and involves simplified and generalized beliefs about a group of people. Using a stereotype, for example that someone is a woman or that another is from India, gives us the impression that we know lots about someone just by knowing one piece of data about him or her. That certainly is efficient, even if it vastly oversimplifies variation within a group and mistakenly attributes perceived group characteristics to an individual.

As with the police category, on the basis of our life experiences we develop a number of implicit theories, coherent and organized groups of beliefs, including implicit self-theories, implicit relationship theories, implicit leadership theories, even implicit followership theories! These are called 'implicit' because they operate mostly below our consciousness and through those speedy brain processes, although we can become aware of them.

Like a stereotype, an implicit leadership theory is triggered almost automatically in leadership-relevant situations, such as hearing that you're getting a new boss, evaluating manager candidates, reacting to a candidate for political office or being introduced to a CEO. Implicit leadership theories then act as schemas, influencing a wide range of leadership-related thoughts and behaviours (Lord and Maher, 1993).

Content of implicit leadership theories

What kinds of information does an implicit leadership theory give you? Aspects of an implicit leadership theory include:

- what leadership is (eg derived from leadership position, charismatic, visionary);
- leader prototypes (description of a typical and/or ideal leader);
- how leaders behave (specific behaviours that a leader would, or wouldn't, engage in);
- whether leadership is born or made and, related to that, whether people can increase their leadership ability or have a stable, fixed amount of leadership;
- leadership identity (beliefs about whether one is a leader or not).

I often begin a leadership workshop or graduate leadership class by asking participants to gauge their agreement or disagreement with some typical beliefs about leadership such as:

- Leadership is natural; leaders are mostly born, not made.
- Leaders are charismatic, confident, strong and extraverted.
- To be a leader, you need a leadership position/role and power over others.
- To become a better leader, you need to work on your leadership weaknesses.
- Whether organizations succeed or fail is mostly due to organizational leadership.

We always have lively discussions and informal debates about these premises, with most participants agreeing at least somewhat with each statement. We sometimes have to dig a little deeper than their conscious, socially desirable responses to get at those hidden assumptions that leaders are born and so on. Even though experienced managers often 'know' better, for example that people can learn to be better leaders, they often reluctantly admit to believing that leadership comes more naturally to some than to others, that it really helps to have a charismatic and confident personality, and that someone with a leadership role is more a leader than someone without a leadership role. In my 30 years of leadership development in the United States and the UK, with thousands of very diverse women and men, I've found very few people who didn't believe that to strengthen their leadership they needed to overcome their leadership weaknesses.

After discussion of each premise, I share insights based on extensive leadership research in each area.

Leadership is natural; leaders are mostly born, not made

My response to this is usually 'Yes and no'. While research has not identified a 'leadership trait' or 'leader personality', there do seem to be a few relatively small genetic and temperamental influences on leadership. Studying identical twins, both male and female, researchers have concluded that about 30 per cent of what contributes to leadership can be attributed to genetic influences, leaving roughly 70 per cent developed by formal and informal life experiences (Arvey et al, 2006; Arvey et al, 2007).

Along with life learning influencing leadership, comprehensive analyses of management/leadership development interventions over 20 years find considerable evidence that people who participate in leadership development do become more effective leaders (Collins and Holton, 2004). More recent analyses of leadership development programmes reveal a moderate to strong impact from these programmes on both leader and organizational effectiveness (eg Avolio, Avey and Quisenberry, 2010). In other words, there's lots of evidence that leader development works.

A very powerful and enduring aspect of whether we believe leadership is natural is our response to the question, 'Can leadership be increased?' Assuming that leadership is an innate trait is described as an 'entity' leadership belief, while assuming that people can actually increase their leadership ability is described as 'incremental' (Dweck, 2006). These beliefs seem innocuous, but whether we lean towards entity or towards incremental leadership beliefs has significance for our leader identity and leader self-efficacy, especially when our leadership is challenged. More about that later.

Leaders are charismatic, confident, strong and extraverted

While our leader prototype may integrate the best of Desmond Tutu, Mother Theresa, Mahatma Gandhi and Winston Churchill, research indicates that charisma is just one potential quality of leadership and that it can be used for good or for selfish purposes. Leaders often need to inspire people, but a leader can be inspirational without being charismatic. Think of Bill Gates, Rowan Williams or Steve Jobs. Leader self-confidence, or leader self-efficacy, is a powerful influence on leadership effectiveness, however. I'm sure you've noticed that people who speak up in groups are more likely to be recognized as leaders by others than those who are quieter.

When we hear people talk about leaders, it's pretty clear that we have levels of leader prototypes, ranging from the global 'leader vs non-leader' category to classification of different types of leaders – military, religious and political leaders, for example – to leader subtypes, like political leaders of a given party (Lord, Foti and De Vader, 1984). These enable us to classify people in leadership at a fairly sophisticated level while still operating out of our implicit leadership theories.

To be a leader, you need a leadership position/role and power over others

It certainly helps – but doesn't make someone a leader. We've all known people in positions of authority who couldn't lead their way out of a paper bag – and people without formal roles who were widely recognized as organizational leaders. Recent research on 'everyday leadership', leadership that brings people together and motivates them to work towards common goals, reveals informal leaders in communities, behind social movements (eg Martin, 2006) and at every level of organizations (Raelin, 2003).

To become a better leader, you need to work on your leadership weaknesses

It makes common sense to address our weaknesses in any important area of life, but we can improve our leadership most by strengthening, and using, our leadership strengths. Positive psychology research has discovered that strengthening our strengths gives us a far better return on the investment of time and energy than working on our weaknesses. We're also likelier to be satisfied and productive when our job responsibilities are matched to our strengths (eg Buckingham and Clifton, 2001; Rath, 2007). But what about weaknesses, you ask? My rule of thumb has been, 'Address your weakness when it interferes with you employing your strengths.'

Whether organizations succeed or fail is mostly due to organizational leadership

This belief, called 'the romance of leadership' (Meindl, Ehrlich and Dukerich, 1985), is very widespread in Western society, where we ascribe great responsibility for organizational outcomes to the individual(s) at the top and neglect the contributions of employees, the context and other situational factors. The romance of leadership is an implicit assumption in executive 'head-hunting', when organizations search for new leaders to turn around their organizations, and in the practice of firing the coach when the team has a bad season or two. It also gives far too much credit – or blame – to individuals for organizational outcomes.

But, sad to say, my students' and workshop participants' implicit leadership beliefs are not easily swayed by my presentation of research evidence. Since implicit leadership theories operate as schemas, information that fits tends to be easily accepted while we disregard/explain away evidence that doesn't tie with our beliefs. Implicit leadership theories tend to be resilient and perseverate, until and unless we deliberately channel our thinking into new views of leadership. Openness to our experiences, such as working with a boss who's different from what we expect bosses to be but seems to be successful at what he/she is doing, can help us shift aspects of our implicit leadership theories as well.

How do we learn implicit leadership theories – and why are they so persistent?

Implicit leadership theories are both culturally socialized and idiosyncratic, so that we tend to believe what others in our culture do about leadership while also being shaped by our own unique experiences. Implicit leadership theories seem to develop quite early in life (eg Ayman-Nolley and Ayman, 2005; Owen, 2007). Research in the UK finds that children can identify typical leader characteristics (eg bossiness and loudness) yet describe ideal leaders as better listeners, sensitive and inspiring (Owen, 2007).

We absorb leadership beliefs just the way we learn other elements of cultural socialization – from our families, our cultural heritage and our societal institutions. As might be expected, our earliest role models and teachers about leadership are our parents. In fact, people describe an ideal leader's characteristics very similarly to the way they describe their parents' traits – more specifically, their fathers' traits. Surprisingly, this occurs regardless of whether parents are seen positively or negatively, as dedicated or tyrannical (Keller, 1999). Parents are our original leader models, while teachers, religious leaders, sports and media figures, and political leaders also make their contributions to our implicit leadership theories (Popper and Mayseless, 2003).

The GLOBE project (Den Hartog et al, 1999) investigated implicit leadership theories worldwide, using hundreds of researchers from 60 cultures representing all major regions of the world. They found surprisingly clear consensus across cultures about what makes an ideal leader, including qualities like being charismatic and visionary, having integrity, and being team-oriented, participative and diplomatic. However, the way the characteristics were translated into behaviour differed between cultures. We all agree that we want our leaders to have integrity, for instance, but what constitutes integrity may well differ from culture to culture.

Impact of implicit leadership theories

In the work world and other situations where we encounter leaders or leadership situations, implicit leadership theories are likely to be triggered often. They influence our leadership identity (how much leadership ability we view ourselves as having) and self-confidence, how we behave in leadership situations, our ability to benefit from leadership training, our responses to managers or other authority figures, and our evaluation of ourselves and others as leaders. Let's look at each of these.

Leader identity

Leader identity may start early in life as popularity, when peers like us, and move into influence as others follow our lead. Communication skills have an important role here, as those with more skills get better responses from others and develop a positive leadership trajectory, while those with fewer communication skills don't have the impact they desire and may move to dominating or to withdrawal from group dynamics.

One path to identity as a leader seems to result at least partially from others' treating you as a leader. In a diverse and sizable study of US adolescents in the Washington, DC area, I found that teachers identified students as leaders on the basis of their speech communication skills, involvement in extracurricular activities and high academic achievement. Classmates' nominations significantly overlapped teacher nominations (but they saw more students as leaders than their teachers did).

Malcolm Gladwell (in *Outliers*, 2008) has demonstrated the powerful cumulative impact of being identified as gifted – and given additional training to develop those gifts. Having teachers and classmates view us as leaders increases the likelihood that we'll be appointed or elected to leadership positions in school (or outside school), experiences that will further strengthen our leadership and communication skills. This is one way that many of us come to recognize our leadership abilities.

One implication of this research, confirmed by other studies (eg Kohlhagen and Culp, 2000), is that extracurricular involvement may serve a dual function: participation can strengthen students' leadership skills and leadership identity while providing a showcase for others to see them as leaders. Students who would not be recognized as leaders for their academic achievements can develop and use communication skills to foster teamwork and performance in out-of-school activities like sport, the Scouts, a band, chorus or drama.

Having others view us as leaders does not guarantee that we will recognize our leadership ability, however, though it makes it more likely. We are more likely to claim leader identity if we see some congruence between our view of leaders and our view of ourselves. However, if we are not recognized in childhood and adolescence as leaders, it's less likely that the leadership prototypes we develop will match our view of ourselves, which has consequences for our behaviour in leadership situations.

Leadership behaviour and leader self-efficacy

Leader identity is not just theoretical; it predicts both our leadership self-confidence and our behaviour in potential leadership situations. People who don't think they're smart enough, confident enough, articulate enough or creative enough to be leaders generally seek to avoid leadership roles and leadership initiative. Also, if we don't believe that we have much leadership, we won't have confidence in ourselves to do what leaders need to do.

Alberto Bandura (1997) and others find that self-efficacy, whether a general feeling of competence or a specific ability, predicts positive outcomes better than actual ability does. Leader self-efficacy is our confidence in our ability to do what's necessary to successfully lead a group to a goal (McCormick, Tanguma and Lopez-Forment, 2002). It influences all sorts of behaviours and outcomes, for instance, how wimpy or challenging our goals are, and how motivated, creative, and persistent we are in the face of obstacles to achieve them (Hannah et al, 2008). People with high leader self-efficacy are more willing to take initiatives or assume leadership responsibilities, especially in volunteer settings (eg Chan and Drasgow, 2001). Leader self-efficacy also influences whether others see us as leaders and how confident they are in our leadership.

Confidence can be mistaken for arrogance and, to avoid being perceived as arrogant or egotistical, people, particularly women, sometimes play down their abilities. But leader self-efficacy does not mean boasting or dominating others; it describes a quiet unshakability, calm in the midst of storm, which buffers us from being devastated by setbacks or by doubts as to our ability (eg Burnette, Pollack and Hoyt, 2010).

As we might expect, women's leader self-efficacy is usually found to be lower than that of men with equivalent positions (cf McCormick, Tanguma and Lopez-Forment, 2002). Women have the delicate balancing act of exercising leadership while not violating cultural expectations of women's behaviour, and the consensus-building, empowering style most favoured by women is often not viewed as leadership in the way that a more authoritative, directive style would be. (That style, however, would get her into trouble as being unwomanly!) The degree of conflict depends upon the organization's or group's norms, of course, and there's more conflict between being a woman and being a leader in traditionally masculine organizations.

It also matters whether a woman believes in the entity leadership theory (leadership is a fixed ability) or the incremental theory (leadership can be increased or developed). Research (Burnette, Pollack and Hoyt, 2010) helps us look at the interaction of women's leader self-efficacy and entity versus incremental leadership beliefs. Women were presented with a 'stereotype threat', a situation in which they could potentially fail and thus confirm negative stereotypes about women's leadership. Women with high leader self-efficacy and an incremental belief that they could strengthen their leadership increased their leader self-efficacy after the threat! If women had low leader self-efficacy along with beliefs that they could not 'grow' more leadership, their self-efficacy and self-esteem took a bigger hit after the threatening situation.

Along with leader self-efficacy, our leadership model or prototype will influence how we behave in leadership situations. Much has been made of a leadership sea change in Western cultures in the last few decades from a 'command and control' model to a more empowering, transformational leadership model. But implicit leadership theories, operating as schemas, are relatively resistant to change, so that many managers today are still operating out of that authority-based model of leadership. Many people have incorporated an authoritative, even authoritarian, model of leadership from their fathers and then had that reinforced by managers who came of age after the Second World War. These leadership behaviours have become ingrained as the brain's default mode of functioning, so managers feel more comfortable in enacting the old style of leadership than doing things differently.

Impact of leader training and development

Habitual leadership style partially explains why leadership programmes, though effective, do not reach all of their participants. While programmes often build on previous leadership experience, many assume that managers, especially new ones, are a 'blank slate' upon which the programme will inscribe leadership skills and knowledge. However, as we've seen, participants enter such programmes with their own implicit leadership theories, a leader identity, higher or lower leader self-efficacy, leader prototypes and habitual leadership styles.

In addition, if we've classified ourselves as non-leaders, even otherwise effective leadership training will not seem applicable to us and won't affect us much. Our beliefs, attitudes and behaviours related to leadership are unlikely to change without reflection, critical examination and intentional unlearning. Given the automatic processing of our leadership schemas, focusing our attention on new ways of thinking will be necessary for us to unlearn old thinking or behaviour patterns (eg Magrath, 1997; Senge, 1990).

The human brain's predisposition to 'business as usual' in relation to implicit leadership theories also needs to be addressed in leader training and development. Leadership programmes need to consider, and work with, the content and impact of implicit leadership theories of their participants (eg Schyns et al, 2011).

Leadership perception and evaluation

We classify people as either leaders or non-leaders on the basis of how well they fit our leadership prototype, and respond to them accordingly. To make a long research history short, leader–follower relationships tend to be more satisfying when the leader is perceived as matching the follower's leader prototype.

Another application of implicit leadership theories is when we assess someone's leadership or give them 360° feedback. Experts in leadership measurement and evaluation recognize that responses to leadership assessments reflect as much about raters' implicit leadership theories (especially their leadership prototypes) as about the specific people being evaluated (eg Shondrick, Dinh and Lord, 2010). That's because once we identify someone as a leader, we tend to attribute all the positive characteristics of our leadership prototype to that person. Similarly, if we don't see someone as a leader, we tend not even to recognize what he or she does as leadership since it is inconsistent with our categorization.

The contribution of implicit relationship and followership theories

All that we've said about implicit leadership theories is not meant to imply that these are the only factors influencing leadership attitudes and behaviour. Our implicit beliefs about relationships and about followership are also influential in leadership behaviour and response to others' leadership. That could be the subject of another whole chapter! See my suggestions for further reading on these topics in the references.

Implications of implicit leadership theories for your own and others' leadership

In my 30 years of leadership education and development, I've seen tremendous leader development progress occur when individuals discovered and constructively changed aspects of their implicit leadership theories. Some recommendations:

- *Reflect on your leadership beliefs*, as you may have begun to do while reading this chapter, and identify how they're working for you.

- *Surface your leadership prototype(s)*. Ask yourself questions like, 'What does it take to be a leader?' 'What kinds of behaviours do I call leadership?' 'Where do I recognize leadership in action?' 'What do people I think of as leaders have in common?' 'What behaviours disqualify a person from my leader category?' 'Does my leadership prototype include everyday leaders or is it so narrow that only people in top leadership roles fit in?'

- *Discover your leader identity*. Have you included yourself in your leader category or do you have lots of excuses as to why you're not really a leader? What evidence would an objective person have for your leadership ability? What do your colleagues think? Have you been acting as a leader but secretly feeling like a fake (that's called the *imposter phenomenon*)? Which potential leadership characteristics have you been discounting because you concluded you were not a leader or didn't have leadership potential?

- *Explore your assumptions about whether leadership ability is fixed or can be developed*. While it can be a little scary, opening your mind to the possibility that leadership can be developed offers many more options for your future success and your resilience in difficult or threatening times. Especially for women, claiming your leadership ability, and believing that you can even strengthen it, can offer protection from stereotype threat, those times when others challenge or doubt your leadership. Modern leadership experts believe that everyone has leadership potential that can be developed for the good of organizations and of society.

- *Strengthen your leader self-efficacy*. You're more likely to take initiative to solve a problem, to offer suggestions in a group or to resist a destructive leader when you have high leader self-efficacy. People with high leader self-efficacy are more likely to feel empowered and less likely to feel powerless in potential leadership situations. Albert Bandura found that people strengthen self-efficacy if they practise the behaviour (in this case, leadership), or carefully observe a model (someone they admire as a leader) and then try some of that person's behaviours, or become accountable (ask for feedback on their own leadership), or recognize their increasing comfort in behaving in the new ways.

- *Be open to seeing leadership in new guises.* Whether you're considering a boss whose leadership style doesn't fit your prototype or a teenager with big ideas for reforming society, you can strengthen others' leadership by recognizing and 'granting' them influence. Widening our leadership category to include leaders of different stripes can be very empowering, especially to someone who hasn't thought of him/herself as having leadership ability. I'm reminded of my daughter's distraught reaction when she heard that her new teacher was one the other kids thought was difficult and unfriendly. Squelching my dread of a very traumatic year, I encouraged her to try to find some things she liked about this new teacher. A week later, I asked again how things were going and heard, 'Oh, Mrs... is much nicer than I heard. I even think she likes me.' The following year, she came home complaining that she was going to have the least popular teacher. I asked her what she would do and she said, 'I'm just going to find some things I like about her, just like I did last year.'

Conclusion

Implicit leadership theories, our organized and coherent assumptions about leaders and leadership, have a multi-faceted impact on our leader identity, leadership behaviour, leader self-efficacy, ability to benefit from leadership development, and interactions with others in leadership roles. Surfacing and examining these assumptions in terms of how constructive they are allows us to expand our 'leader' category to include non-stereotypical ways of exercising leadership, develop realistic leader identities, strengthen our leader self-efficacy, take the initiative in leadership situations, and interact more constructively with those in leadership roles in our lives. Those designing leadership development programmes would increase their impact as they assisted participants to work with their own implicit leadership theories.

References

Arvey, RD, Rotundo, M, Johnson, W, Zhang, Z and McGue, G (2006) The determinants of leadership role occupancy: genetic and personality factors, *Leadership Quarterly*, 17 (1), pp 1–20

Arvey, RD, Zhang, Z, Avolio, B and Krueger, RF (2007) Developmental and genetic determinants of leadership role occupancy among women, *Journal of Applied Psychology*, 92 (3), pp 693–706

Avolio, BJ, Avey, JB and Quisenberry, D (2010) Estimating return on leadership development investment, *Leadership Quarterly*, 21 (4), pp 633–44

Ayman-Nolley, S and Ayman, R (2005) Children's implicit theory of leadership, in *Implicit Leadership Theories: Essays and explorations*, ed B Schyns and JR Meindl, pp 189–233, Information Age, Greenwich, Conn

Bandura, A (1997) *Self-efficacy: The exercise of control*, WH Freeman, New York

Buckingham, DO and Clifton, M (2001) *Now, Discover Your Strengths*, Free Press, New York

Burnette, JL, Pollack, JM and Hoyt, CL (2010) Individual differences in implicit leadership theories of leadership ability and self-efficacy, *Journal of Leadership Studies*, 3 (4), pp 46–56

Chan, KY and Drasgow, F (2001) Toward a theory of individual differences and leadership: understanding the motivation to lead, *Journal of Applied Psychology*, 86 (3), pp 481–98

Collins, DB and Holton, EF (2004) The effectiveness of managerial leadership development programs: a meta-analysis of studies from 1982 to 2001, *Human Resource Development Quarterly*, 15, pp 217–42

Den Hartog, N, House, RJ, Hanges, PJ, Ruiz-Quintanilla, SA, Dorfman, PW, Brenk, KM, Konrad, E and Sabadin, A (1999) Culture specific and cross-culturally generalizable implicit leadership theories: are attributes of charismatic/transformational leadership universally endorsed?, *Leadership Quarterly*, 10 (2) 219–56

Dweck, C (2006) *Mindset: The new psychology of success*, Random House, New York

Gladwell, M (2008) *Outliers: The story of success*, Little, Brown and Co, New York

Hannah, ST, Avolio, BJ, Luthans, F and Harms, PD (2008) Leadership efficacy: review and future directions, *The Leadership Quarterly* (2008), 19 (6), pp 669–92

Keller, T (1999) Images of the familiar: individual differences and implicit leadership theories, *Leadership Quarterly*, 10 (4), pp 589–607

Kohlhagen, B and Culp, K (2000) Identifying, defining, applying, analyzing and synthesizing leadership opportunities with adolescents, *Journal of Leadership and Organizational Studies*, 7 (2), pp 50–57

Lord, RG, Foti, RJ and De Vader, CL (1984) A test of leadership categorization theory: internal structure, informational processing, and leadership perceptions, *Organizational Behavior and Human Performance*, 34 (3), pp 343–78

Lord, RG and Maher, KJ (1993) *Leadership and Information Processing: Linking perceptions and performance*, Routledge, New York

Magrath, AJ (1997) The importance of unlearning, *Across the Board*, 34 (2), pp 39–41

Martin, A (2006) *Everyday Leadership*, Center for Creative Leadership (CCL), Colorado Springs, Colo

McCormick, M, Tanguma, J and Lopez-Forment, AS (2002) Extending self-efficacy to leadership: a review and empirical test, *Journal of Leadership Education*, 1 (2), pp 1–15

Meindl, JR, Ehrlich, SB and Dukerich, JM (1985) The romance of leadership, *Administrative Science Quarterly*, 30 (1), pp 78–102

Owen, H (2007) *Creating Leaders in the Classroom: How teachers can develop a new generation of leaders*, Routledge, New York

Popper, M and Mayseless, O (2003) Back to basics: applying a parenting perspective to transformational leadership, *Leadership Quarterly*, 14, pp 41–65

Raelin, JA (2003) *Creating Leaderful Organizations: How to bring out leadership in everyone*, Berrett-Koehler, San Franscisco, Calif

Rath, T (2007) *StrengthsFinder 2.0*, Gallup Press, New York

Schyns, B, Kiefer, T, Kerschreiter, R and Tymon, A (2011) Teaching implicit leadership theories to develop leaders and leadership: how and why it can make a difference, *Academy of Management Learning and Education*, 10 (3), pp 397–408

Senge, P (1990) *The Fifth Discipline: The art and practice of the learning organization*, Doubleday, New York

Shondrick, SJ, Dinh, JE and Lord, RG (2010) Developments in implicit leadership theory and cognitive science: applications to improving measurement and understanding alternatives to hierarchical leadership, *Leadership Quarterly*, 21, pp 959–78

Resources for further study of implicit relationship and implicit followership theories

Implicit relationship theories (eg attachment security)

Harms, PD (2011) Adult attachment styles in the workplace, *Human Resources Management Review*, 21, pp 285–96

Mayseless, O (2010) Attachment and the leader–follower relationship, *Journal of Social and Personal Relationships*, 27 (2), pp 271–80

Implicit followership theories

Ira Chaleff's followership [Online] http://www.courageousfollower.net/ (accessed 1 March 2012)

Followership Learning Community of the International Leadership Association [Online] http://www.ila-net.org/communities/LC/Followership.htm (accessed 30 April 2012)

Sy, T (2010) What do you think of followers? Examining the content, structure, and consequences of implicit followership theories, *Organizational Behavior and Human Decision Processes*, 113 (2), pp 73–84

van Gils, S, van Quaquebeke, N and van Knippenberg, D (2010) The X-factor: on the relevance of implicit leadership and followership theories for leader–member exchange agreement, *European Journal of Work and Organizational Psychology*, 19 (3), pp 333–63

What is leadership development when it is not the personal development of leaders?

05

FIONA KENNEDY

We are making our way back from morning tea on the fourth day of an in-house leadership development programme. I am walking with Mike, one of the 20 participants, when he observes: 'This programme isn't really about personal development is it?' His tone is thoughtful and curious. He is noticing something about what this programme is *not* and in doing so he is asking me to help him with what it *is*. He tells me that in anticipating the programme he had imagined that he would be learning about himself. I heartily agree with him and, in fact, I am a little excited about what he is noticing: 'You are right. This is *not* personal development.' I go on to describe the New Zealand Leadership Institute (NZLI) approach to leadership in terms of work that is held in between people and not by particular bounded individuals. Mike nods along as I talk but all the while he is looking slightly unsure. It seems that he gets 'the gist of it'. He seems to follow me – sort of. I am confirming something that he is becoming aware of but we are both groping around and I am certainly not giving him a repeatable account of this new 'thing'.

Mike's questioning was unusual in that he had tried to put words around something that was identifiable mostly by what it wasn't (*Not personal development of leaders*). However, on reflection, it seemed to me that his curiosity about what leadership development *is* when it is not understood and treated as personal development was not unusual. The slightly murky feel of the terrain he was experiencing and our conversation did not seem unusual either. I suspected that he was giving voice to questions that were lurking for many of our participants.

So I would like to address Mike's question: 'What is leadership development when it is *not* about developing individual leaders?' and along with that to address what it means when we say that leadership is not the province of special individuals, but rather arises in between people. For leadership development that is *not* primarily about developing individuals does make for strange, somewhat murky territory, particularly in comparison with traditional accounts of leadership and leadership development. As Mike was noticing there are important differences between leadership development that proceeds from the assumption that 'leadership exists in between people' and development that follows conventional assumptions about the location of leadership. In addressing this question it is important to draw attention to some of the traditional and taken-for-granted assumptions that pull against emerging approaches to leadership. This is because part of the work in developing leadership that can meet the needs of contemporary circumstances involves becoming aware of the tug and pull of established assumptions and their pervasive effects.

Why is it hard to grasp leadership as existing in between people?

Mike had expected a leadership programme that focused on personal development for himself and his colleagues. His assumption was that leadership development involved the personal development of people in formal leadership roles. Expectations related to this assumption had endured despite many signals that, in this programme, this was not the case. Strong signals about the nature of the development work had begun even before facilitators and participants came together for the first time. For example, pre-programme material that had been sent to participants had highlighted the dynamic, multi-sided nature of leadership work and had not focused on the personal development of individual leaders at all. We had also addressed this issue directly with Mike and his colleagues from the very beginning of our work together. So, why might Mike's expectations that leadership development be about the personal development of individuals have persisted?

First, it would probably be fair to say that Mike's expectations were absolutely in sync with assumptions about leadership that surrounded him and that shape expectations about leadership, without people ever pausing to think about those expectations or to really notice them. This is because talk of leadership invariably slips towards a focus on particular people, often those who have a position of institutional power and/or those who stand out from the rest. Historically leadership stories revolve around noteworthy individuals, and definitions of leadership generally relate to an individual who brings people together to achieve their goals. While there are numerous definitions of leadership, they tend to have one thing in common – they focus on an individual who influences others in such a way as to be called a leader. Indeed William Drath has combed existing definitions of leadership. He cites six particularly authoritative definitions and asks: 'What is the same about these?' He points out that each definition takes up the very same fundamental perspective. That is, leadership involves one special person (the leader) who influences others (the followers). It stands to reason, then, that leadership development would focus on advancing the qualities possessed by those who stand out, bring people together and influence things. From this perspective it was not at all strange that Mike would anticipate a conventional approach to leadership development. What was remarkable was that he was questioning his expectations.

Second, in everyday talk the relationship between leadership and development is equally committed to the individual. Those who have the opportunity to participate in leadership development are almost always people in formal leadership roles. Furthermore the study of human development is full of theories about how individuals grow and develop. Theories of human development that have influenced leadership development focus on how individuals develop as bounded beings as they interact with the world. For example Maslow's hierarchy of needs or Jung's ideas about individuation from developmental psychology offer different ways of conceptualizing human development. However, what is the same about both theories is that they firmly privilege the distinct, separate individual. In organizations, ideas about leadership development are frequently linked to individual development plans and the development of individual competencies, habits or attributes. In fact, in performance development, the front and centre positioning of the individual goes without saying. While it is understood that there is always a context for leadership at work, the individual is the subject of these conversations and assessments. The context becomes the background, sometimes completely whited out, inferred or referenced in vague, impressionistic strokes.

So what constitutes leadership and development has been weighted heavily in an individual direction. From this perspective Mike's puzzlement made absolute sense because 'reading the waters' he was noticing things that did not fit with what he 'knew'. While from an intellectual point of view he might have appreciated the distinctions we had made in orienting him and his colleagues to the programme, he would still have to contend with much more established assumptions all around him, ones that he knew 'in his bones' and that were being reinforced at every turn. Historic, traditional ways of thinking about leadership draw attention towards, individual leaders, and leadership development is associated with theories of how individuals grow and with interest in the attributes of individual leaders.

All of this does not disappear just because a development programme, such as the one Mike was encountering, is based on different assumptions. While the limitations of historic ways of thinking may be apparent and ideas like collective or shared leadership may be appealing, at least in the West we are inclined to see and imagine leadership *and* it's development as a powerfully individual construct. Therefore, while my explanation probably fitted with Mike's practical sense of what we were up to, it was also strange and dissonant, being out of tune with a wealth of established understandings that were buzzing in the background, alive and well. While Mike followed along as I talked about leadership development being something other than the personal development of leaders, what this meant seemed to continually slip just out of view. It was as if our conversation was going along nicely, but with muffled words.

In inching beyond muffled words I have found it helpful to put *relationships* and *conversations* as absolutely front and centre to explanations of leadership development work. Development work that holds relationships and conversations as fundamental is quite distinct from development work that is individually focused, and is built from quite different assumptions about the social world. While in practice relationships and conversation are hard to separate from one another, I address each in turn here.

Relationships as the basis for leadership

As I have already suggested, traditional ways of talking about leadership and its development often depict leadership without the particulars of its context, or show the context as relatively non-specific and in the background. For example, popular writing is somewhat obsessed with identifying the characteristics, skills or habits of successful leaders, while in organizations leadership may be identified in predetermined ways such as through identified competencies and 360° evaluations. The myriad threads that make up moments of leadership and the dynamics that bring them together or that contribute to the experience of leadership remain very crudely drawn. Indeed, managers who receive low 360° feedback ratings are usually quick to point out some vital particulars that have shaped their relational situation and that have no place in the rating scales that form the core of most 360° feedback reports. However, in making the particulars of context visible after the fact, managers invariably seem defensive. It is as if bringing visibility to a relational context is already a sign of weak leadership. It becomes of interest only in the absence of leadership or when problems arise.

The consequences of implying that understanding and developing leadership does not require working with the particulars of contexts are costly. As Ron Heifitz and his colleagues have pointed out, contemporary social issues are complex and often intractable, requiring communities to become actively involved with the problems that affect them. Individual constructs of leadership, such as those represented in 'measures' of leadership that by definition do not value the particularities of people and their stories, depict the work of leadership as an exercise in individual skill and competence. In doing so, direct reports, community members and citizens are tacitly excused from fully engaging with the problems that affect them.

Working with leadership as a relational construct calls for a much more vivid, immediate and particular rendering of the context. In fact, relational leadership assumes that it is impossible not to be in relationships with others and that there is no such thing as a context-free individual. This means that the focus of attention shifts from the beliefs, thoughts and actions of individuals in leadership roles to the relational responses that are emerging between people in the present. This is an important and fundamental shift. The location for development work is not in the individual but in relationships, because what is understood or experienced as leadership comes to life between people. One way of thinking about this is that attention is drawn away from bounded individuals to the sense and shape of things in an ongoing social situation. For example, in the conversation with Mike we would not be so focused on Mike's individual characteristics – such as his capacity to ask good questions – but on what was emerging between Mike and me as we responded to one another. For as we went along together we were creating realities that are a great deal more complex than the acts or attributes of either of us. Our conversation was buoyed along by a climate of curiosity and discovery that we produced together, enabling us to hang in with not knowing and to allow space for things to remain unclear.

Indeed, leadership development work that aims to work with the complexity of relational leadership focuses on movement and meaning. For example, a manager with low 360° feedback ratings would not be asked to focus on what caused his or her ratings or what he or she planned to do to change things but to notice how he or she responds in ongoing conversation with others, particularly those who have contributed to the feedback. In fact, a relational perspective has implications for profiling and psychometric approaches to leadership. Many of these approaches are not helpful to developing relational leadership. This is because they imply that styles of response or levels of competence are fixed and individual, thereby completely missing the dynamics of what goes on and emerges in between people as well as potentially restricting possibilities for how people might make sense of themselves in the future.

Holding relationships as the basic starting point for leadership development offers very fertile ground for in-house development programmes. Mike and his colleagues can be seen as having opportunities for creating the relationships that till the soil for leadership within their organization. As I have noted above, holding relationships as central to leadership means that leadership work is shared work. Therefore it is no longer tenable to treat responsibility for leadership as residing within a few individuals who are identified as leaders. When possibilities for leadership are in between people, then problems in leadership must also be understood from a relational perspective. For example Mike and his colleagues argued that short-term thinking and overbearing senior management inhibited leadership in their organization. A relational perspective involves considering the ongoing dynamic of situations as they are created and recreated between people in the moment. Therefore some of the work for Mike's group involved questioning the sort of identities they were creating for themselves as they talked about this dynamic in their business. Their work included considering how their ways of thinking and talking kept this problematic dynamic alive, how it served to persuade them that their leadership work could not begin until after their senior team had changed!

Leadership through conversation

I have argued that relational processes are the location for leadership development work. This is a radical departure from associating leadership with special individuals and it requires quite different ways of thinking about the work of leadership. Relational leadership requires working with the dynamic territory *in between* people and this territory is shaped through conversations. Conversations 'carry' the nuances and possibilities of how people frame, reframe and respond to leadership problems. That is why conversation is such important leadership work. As evolutionary biologist Humberto Maturana puts it, through conversation *'we bring forth a world'*.

However, this perspective calls for a fundamental shift in how conversations are valued and practised in leadership work. Developing conversational practices flies in the face of common understandings and beliefs about business, where conversation is often under-valued or even directly devalued. Devaluing conversation can be subtle; it is often light-hearted enough to make serious challenges seem churlish and it is pervasive. For example, Elvis Presley's song *A little less conversation* starts with those words and continues with the refrain: 'a little less conversation, a little more action please'. In Aotearoa, New Zealand, we have a saying that mixes Maori and European languages, 'We need less hui [the Maori word for meeting] and more do-ey', while a Chinese proverb warns: 'Talk doesn't cook rice.' Indeed this theme of: 'don't talk, just do' reminds me of my late grandmother who used to find my work with organizations baffling and irritating. She would snap: 'But what do you *do*?'

One of the problems with these common understandings is that the two states – 'hui' and 'do-ey' – are held as quite distinct and separate. They are constructed as if talk and action must occur in a sequence. First conversation happens and then the action. When talk is seen as being in a linear relationship to action, it follows that the action cannot even begin until the talking stops. Talking is a prelude to – and by definition lesser than – action. Furthermore, from my grandmother' or Elvis's perspective, conversation can actually be an impediment to action. All of these expressions contribute to a view of conversation as being in a linear, and at times antagonistic, relationship with action. In a world where leadership is seen as influencing people to achieve their goals and where conversation is seen as an impediment to action, conversation becomes a most unlikely company for leadership!

Devaluing conversation also has spin-off effects that can effectively block leadership work. For example, when conversation is seen as antagonistic to action, reflecting on organizational conversational processes is unlikely to be considered valid or important leadership work. Under these circumstances Mike and his colleagues might not take time to reflect on their conversations and so might never see how they themselves sustain problematic leadership dynamics in their organization. They might remain unaware of how they are creating all sorts of colour, drama and emotional energy for the story of overbearing, short-sighted senior managers, and how this story absolves them of leadership responsibility, implying that problems lie wholly beyond their reach – above them in the organizational hierarchy. Similarly, a manager with low 360° ratings may become caught in a discussion of whether the feedback was fair or not or may argue that things have changed, rather than becoming aware of conversational patterns that sustain problematic perceptions of his or her leadership in the present.

Therefore viewing conversation as important work requires shifting focus and becoming alert to possibilities as they are evolving in the present, rather than being oriented to change and time as linear phenomena. However, doing this can feel strange, particularly in the context of organizations where explaining the past or planning the future has taken the lion's share of managerial attention. A focus on conversation goes against this tide by making the present, and what is being brought to life in the present moment, vitally important. As Kenneth Gergen writes: '[We] stand each moment at a precious juncture... we may sustain tradition but we are also free to innovate and transform' (2009: 49). As I discussed with regard to the relationship between Mike, his colleagues and their senior management team, those junctures are alive with possibility and choices. In addition, multiple layers of meaning are alive in any conversation. Indeed, Ralph Stacey suggests that conversations are alive at six levels, including the conscious and unconscious, formal and informal, legitimate and shadow (Stacey, 2001).

Holding conversation as important work also means unsettling assumptions about how meaning evolves and is managed in leadership. The proposition that we are at a 'precious juncture' where we are perpetually constructing things assumes that meaning is unstable. This is quite at odds with established ways of work and the assumptions that underlie them. In many organizations, or in leadership roles, managers may spend time poring over presentations or crafting written communication, planning things and treating communication as a *tool* for transmitting ideas and information. This perspective assumes that meaning can be relatively stable and that leadership work involves achieving accuracy or effectiveness in communication.

Psychometric profiles and other tools that help managers to see themselves contribute to this perspective by implying that selves are stable and can be defined. However, leadership development that is not personal development is likely to hold psychometric profiling or 360° feedback very lightly – or even at arm's length – because these methods subtly reinforce an individual view of the leadership terrain and potentially restrict new possibilities in the present.

Relational leadership development

In this chapter I have attempted to address Mike's question: What is the nature of leadership development when it is not about individual personal development? I have emphasized some of the embedded, pervasive and subtle assumptions and 'truths' that steer us back to an individual view of leadership. I have done so in the hope that making some of these assumptions visible will help get beyond muffled words. In particular I hope that recognizing those assumptions will enable new ideas about leadership to get some traction so that they are not doused out the minute they encounter challenges from more traditional forms of thought. Conversations that occurred later in Mike's leadership development programme illustrate the push and pull of conventional ideas about leadership and relational leadership practice:

> It is just past midway through the programme. Key members of the organization's senior team who are not part of the programme have joined the participants for the morning to talk about leadership in the organization. Colin, the most senior of the visiting managers, has moved effortlessly into a role where he alone is holding the floor. In fact almost before we know it, Colin is steaming full speed ahead and the possibility of conversation seems like the idealistic stuff of a development programme! Like a scene from *Alice in Wonderland*, Mike and his colleagues actually seem to become smaller as Colin steams on. In the blink of an eye the visiting senior managers are growing bigger and bigger while Mike and his colleagues shrink. I feel my heart sinking.
>
> Then, as Colin pauses for breath, one of Mike's colleagues leans forward. She addresses Colin in a quiet, thoughtful manner saying: 'You know I really have to disagree with you about that.' Then Mike moves quickly into the little opening she has created. He says: 'Perhaps it would be useful for us to look at other ways of doing things? There are so many good options available. We could do so much more.'
>
> Gradually the balance of conversation begins to shift. Colin continues to speak more than others but importantly, he is no longer 'holding the floor'. Now for 90 minutes the conversation ranges widely and includes an agreement to totally re-think traditional ways of approaching sales and marketing in the

organization. Challenges and questions move back and forth between Mike and his colleagues as well as between the programme participants and the visiting senior managers. At some point Colin assures them: 'We absolutely need you guys. The organization cannot develop without you.'

Hours later as we walk to our cars with our boxes and suitcases, Mike and I talk again. He muses: 'This programme is not about personal development and yet I feel different about myself and my role at work and I think differently about it.' 'How so?' I ask. 'Well,' he tells me, 'I don't know. I guess I ask a lot more questions. That's just one little thing but it seems to make a difference.' 'What difference?' I ask. 'Aaah...' Now it is his turn to grope around. 'It's just that people seem to respond to questions, so, it changes things up somehow or other.' He shrugs – moves to say more and doesn't. We smile wryly and go our separate ways.

As Kenneth Gergen writes: '[We] stand each moment at a precious juncture... we may sustain tradition but we are also free to innovate and transform.' When Colin entered the room we were all for a time captured in ways that left us mute. Perhaps Colin and his way of being with others stimulated traditional anticipations of leadership, where leadership is about particular individuals. In any event, compared with Colin the rest of us immediately became 'followers'. Colin became exemplary while also satisfying well-worn stories about overbearing leaders in Mike's organization. However, some of the participants recognized this trap, and recognizing the trap for what it was was vital for their motivation and skill in getting them out of it. They were able to see, in Gergen's language, that they were in fact 'free to innovate and transform'. While words like 'transform' sound grand, exercising their responsibility to speak, to begin challenging the narrative of overbearing senior managers and to be involved in the future of the organization was transformative in that moment.

Habits of separating talking and doing – 'hui' and 'do-ey' – can enable us to sustain old problematic stories because we are able to deny what we *do* when we talk. Appreciating the relationship between leadership and conversation helped programme participants to see what they were *doing* and the story they inhabited when Colin and other senior managers joined them. It helped them disrupt this narrative of overbearing senior managers with its sub-themes about power and powerlessness so that they could get involved in important decisions about the organization's future. Indeed, leadership development that is not personal development asks participants to consider the world that they are creating and the stories they chose to perpetuate or disrupt in their involvements with others in the here and now. That is exactly what Mike and his colleagues did.

Finally, when Mike attempted to speak about the relationship between personal development and leadership development, he didn't get very far without putting the changes he was experiencing into a relational context. When I asked what was different, he sparked up his sense of that by recalling himself in relationship with others at work. I don't know what led us both to smile and head back to our respective home cities rather than pursuing Mike's original assertion that he himself had changed and that therefore perhaps our work had been 'personal development'. However, I like to think we smiled because when asked what was different he had located his differences by seeing himself with others and invoking something new that was occurring *in between* people. As he did so, thinking about leadership development in terms that were not thoroughly embedded in a particular context seemed increasingly less plausible.

References

Stacey, R (2001) *Complex Responsive Processes in Organizations: Learning and knowledge creation*, Routledge, London
Gergen, K (2009) *Relational Being*, Oxford University Press, New York

Leadership reflections

06

WARREN BENNIS

Note from the Editor

Too many more years ago than I care to remember, I worked in marketing for a well-known corporate organization. I had been interested in leadership since school and came across a book by Warren Bennis. A few years later I met him at a conference in London. We talked and have stayed in touch. Understanding leadership took over my life, and meeting Warren at Harvard with others to discuss whether leadership could be taught was a highlight of my life. When planning this book, it was a natural thing to ask Warren to contribute and it was agreed that the best way was for him to talk about leadership as part of his own life rather than his life studies of others. Therefore, it seems appropriate that before moving to the second part of the book, which is rich with examples of what is happening to leadership around the world, Warren's contribution acts as a bridge between the challenges (the first part of the book) and what is happening.

Warren Bennis

I know the way my life has been enriched and how my own development has been about conversations, relationships and connections I've had with others. I don't quarantine myself and suddenly shout 'Eureka!' All of my learning comes through others – meaning that I thrive and grow and learn *through* others, *with* others, and *through* conversation and through good questions.

Touching people with my writing and teaching is what counts most for me.

I have co-taught a course for the past 13 years with University of Southern California's former University President, Dr Steven Sample. The course is called 'The Art and Adventure of Leadership' – *not* 'The Art and the Science', by the way. The first few years we didn't know quite what direction to take and how we could organize a semester-long course about a *portmanteau* topic like leadership. Eventually, over the years, the course began stirring up a campus buzz, and in the last semester we taught it, nearly 300 students applied for 42 openings. The course has become totemic on campus. In the last several years some students have applied to USC hoping to get admitted to the course when they became juniors or seniors.

So over 13 years 500 or so students have taken the course. The students have organized two reunions over the years, and over those weekends we hear their stories about how what they have learned has been incarnated in their life stories. They come from all over the world, a few from as far as Iraq and Uganda, for that weekend, combined of course – hey, this is USC – with a football Saturday.

One of the reasons teaching is so rewarding is that with first-rate, challenging minds, you just can't help learning. I know that sounds clichéd – but it's true. The second reason is that in conversations with my students, I feel I've become a master teacher. That feeling of mastery is ineffable. I don't feel that way about my writing or just about anything else. I don't know exactly what I do that makes it that way but for me it's an elixir, a goad to keep learning and working at it; and, yes, a continuing love affair, living the life of the mind. Now, by the way, I love it when people read a book of mine and say, 'I learned something important that is going to stay with me forever.' I don't know how to put it in a non-clichéd way but to be able to influence the kinds of choices people are going to make in their lives and to bring out their 'better angels'? What could be more fulfilling than that? Here I am at 85 with a terrific day-job. Where else could that happen? I love the title of Nobel Laureate Richard Feynman's book, *The Pleasure of Finding Things Out*. That's what it's all about, isn't it?

The philosopher Habermas talks about *possible selves*, which always brings to mind an interview with an extraordinary man, John Gardner, another valued mentor. Most people 50 years or younger don't know the name John Gardner. I'm not talking about the novelist; I'm talking about Lyndon Johnson's Secretary of Health, Education, and Welfare (HEW) back when it was one of the most important and largest cabinet posts. John Gardner, from humble origins, a Roman Catholic, a conservative, his essential character, not his politics: reserved, low-keyed, and with a capacity for long, thoughtful and comfortable silences. He was the only Republican in

President Johnson's cabinet. He had a brilliant career that included founding the White House Fellowship programme as well as Common Cause and Independent Sector.

Bob Thomas and I interviewed him for our book, *Geeks and Geezers*. We interviewed about 45 successful leaders, Geeks (32 years and younger) and Geezers (70 years and older). John was 86 when I sat down with him on the lush, green campus of Stanford in 2001. I loved our conversation, about two and a half hours that went like five minutes. He'd been a mentor for many years: mentoring across far distances with phone calls, before e-mail, with real letters and occasional meetings in Washington. We weren't close, like I was with Doug McGregor, but he was the guy I would call and say, 'John what do you think?' I remember asking him, 'John, how did you get *here* from *there*?' At that time, he was a famous, best-selling and influential author, a mentor to hundreds of people. He looked puzzled for a minute and then he said, after one of his longer-than-usual silences, 'There were, I guess, some qualities there that life was waiting to pull out of me.' Boy, can I identify with that: *what life is waiting to pull out of us.* Just how, I wonder to this day, how do we get to know all our possible selves?

Looking back, I wanted to be like my mentor Doug McGregor, who was a college president. I wanted that almost desperately, probably too much. I figured if I wanted to be a college president I had better take on some administrative office. Which is why I left a full professorship at MIT, with an office overlooking the Charles River. I threw my hat into every damn available ring, so to speak, and sought a provostship (head of a college) as a stepping stone for a presidency. (Very, very UN-academic!) That would be a start, I thought, which led to four years as provost at SUNY/Buffalo. My colleagues at MIT were baffled, and I recall one colleague consoling me with a miserable attempt at empathy, referring to my decision, with mild condescension, as a 'mid-career' crisis.

I often admired my MIT dean at faculty meetings. He would make a speech, say at a banquet for donors or a faculty meeting, take no more than seven or eight minutes, and they were always witty, resonant and relevant. He would finish and I sat there in thought, 'Oh my God, I could never do that.' When I was suddenly a provost, guess what: I was asked to give speeches and discovered, 'Hey I can do that.' That was one of those selves that seemed congruent with Warren Bennis. In a way I chose something that 'pulled out' some quality of me. I started giving quick, witty, even resonant speeches. How would I know if I hadn't tried? How would I know that was one of lurking 'possible selves'?

Now here is the tricky part of 'What is authentic?' And here I need to talk about somebody I wrote about: Al Gore. I have a deep admiration and affection for our former Vice President. To go out on the limb, a shaky one at that, I believe that he's an exemplar of someone who was a hostage of his parents' dream: that one day 'our Al' will and should be a US president. From early on in his youth, he was virtually brought up to be president, from where he was sent to school and even how he dressed. I have wondered to this day whether he really, *really* wanted to be president. Notice how he comes across these days, especially since his book *An Inconvenient Truth* was published, followed quickly by winning the Nobel Peace Prize. His concern about deforestation and the environment is where his heart is, where he seems totally relaxed and comfortable in his own skin, not in his parents' bespoke suits. Compare his performances in those painful-to-watch TV debates with George W. Bush in the 2000 presidential campaign. I often show clips of that TV debate to my class and squirm every time. To repeat myself, I think the Al Gore I know, the guy you would love to have a beer with, simply didn't want that job enough. That led to a less real Al Gore. When you're with Al Gore today, with a group of people, friends, colleagues, he is comfortable, witty and, on top of that, brilliant. This is the authentic and remarkable person I know, not the political Al Gore who ran for president over a decade ago.

One more thing, if I may. As I said earlier, my wife is a retired psycho-pharmacologist and I've picked up a few useful psychoanalytic terms from her. She would say, if the role you choose (or find yourself in) is congruent with at least one of those possible selves, it is *ego-syntonic*. On the other hand, if the role you are playing is not congruent with who you are, the 'real me' as William James described it, that's *ego-dystonic*. It became clear to me that I was fortunate enough to end up in roles that pulled from me the person I really wanted to be:

Distinguished Professor Warren Bennis.

PART II
The transformation of leadership

Latin America
In search of collaborative approaches to leadership

07

JESUS SAMPEDRO HIDALGO

The title of this chapter encapsulates the main idea of a region redefining its scheme of how leaders and followers interact from a boss-dependent to a more collaborative one. The central notion of the chapter refers to a reality that has to cope with the interactive processes being constantly interrupted by power-concentrating bosses who control decisions, stand in the path of collective effort, and slow down the regular organizational flow. One of the emerging paradigms in the Latin American organizational world gravitates around 'Cool-laboration', an idea that entails turning to and fostering collaborative environments that may enhance individual and group significance (connecting talents productively in the long term), building more flexibility into operations (rather than bureaucracy), and fostering innovation (to take advantage of people's creative capacity).

Leadership in Latin America

Latin America in the modern era has been known for the constant disruptions of its developmental and democratic systems. The battles between settlers and natives for dominion that started more than 500 years ago created over the centuries a dynamic force that has shaped the way communication, respect, tolerance, communal life and leader–follower interaction are manifest. This culture has produced a patriarchal sense of leadership that followers somehow agree and depend upon. According to McIntosh and Irving (2010), 'the predominant leadership style in Latin America coming from the Spanish conquest, continuing through the colonial and early independence periods, and extending to today is *caudillaje* or *caudillismo*.' Usually *caudillaje* is defined in relationship to dictatorship. Hamill (1992), quoted by McIntosh and Irving, reported that the word *caudillo* comes from the Latin *capitellum*, the diminutive of *caput* or head. The *caudillo* is the sole head of the entity he leads. This kind of leadership can be seen as a style of life where domination is exercised by one man, the *caudillo*. According to Hamill, another term often used in the literature on Latin America is *cacique*; this most often refers to a *caudillo* on a more local level such as a town or particular organization, while the *caudillo* operates on a broader stage such as an area of the country or the country itself. McIntosh and Irving refer to Chevalier quoting the 1729 definition of *cacique* from the *Spanish Dictionary of the Royal Academy*: 'The first of his village or the republic, the one with more authority or power and who because of his pride wants to make himself feared and obeyed by all of his inferiors' (McIntosh and Irving, 2010: 30).

Naturally, this leadership style has permeated through the organizational walls and has made its influence felt in the corporate hallways. However, the despotic, authoritative and patriarchal leadership dynamics present in Latin America's reality are beginning to fade. Romeo (2004) conducted an introductory study with the Business Association of Latin American Studies (BALAS), Iberoamerican Academy of Management and the Academy of Management's International Division on whether countries tended more toward the *patron* (a term also used to refer to the previously mentioned notion of a boss or leader) or towards the modern, more participative style; the results lead him to see the emerging possibility of a significant shift in contemporary Latin American leadership from the *patron* style to modern leadership.

Followers are awakening to the possibilities and benefits of a more participatory, inclusive and synergistic style. There is evidence, at least in the last two decades, that some leaders have started a reforming process within the organizational realm in the way leadership is conceived and practised. This notion has focused on efforts to transform leadership into a form that is more respectful and open, less despotic and rigid, narrower in its power distance and wider in its appreciation for people's concerns. An era of innovation and the prospect of a globalized future demand a more collaborative space, where the many creative ideas that emerge may flow more productively and lead the Latin American region to engage in the global economy. Although this will not occur overnight, the evidence shows signs of growing maturity on the part of emerging leaders and glimpses of a marketplace transformation.

The transforming status

One of the main issues to deal with in the region is that Latin Americans seem to accept a leadership approach that concentrates power in a person. Its long-lasting existence confirms that people seem to view it as legitimate (regardless of the mechanisms through which it was obtained), which is a necessary condition for any leadership style to be accepted. However, various studies show evidence of a transition from a power-concentrating leadership style to a power-distributing one.

For example, a study done in Venezuela by Granell in 1997 assessed the Venezuelan management style on a continuum between authoritarian and participatory features, particularly from the perspective of the interviewed workers. Interestingly enough it was found that in real-life working relationships, the bosses' management style was often (55 per cent of the cases) authoritarian. Nevertheless, according to the study, a large majority (75 per cent) of workers preferred to work under a more participatory style. Intrinsically, Venezuelans tend to show a leadership style that is 'eccentric' and seeks some kind of public recognition from others (Márquez and De Avellán, 2008). Gustavo Cisneros, owner of the biggest media conglomerate in the region, considers that Venezuela is a country with a high awareness of social status and authoritarian leadership styles (Marquardt and Berger, 2000). But such descriptions cannot be generalized among all Venezuelans and should not be considered exclusive to Venezuela, as other countries in the region display similar characteristics.

In October 2011 Odir Pereira, Director of the Brazilian Institute of Leadership, took part in a study involving 462 Brazilian leaders, entitled 'How Brazilian executives see themselves and their organizations'. The major finding was that Brazilians prefer paternalistic and authoritative styles of leadership rather than participative ones (Pereira, 2011). Table 7.1 shows that workers, in particular, prefer such a style.

More interesting conclusions were drawn in 2010 in Boston, at the International Leadership Association (ILA) world conference, where a round-table discussion led by Laura Santana from the Center for Creative Leadership

TABLE 7.1   Preferred styles of leadership among Brazilian workers and MBAs

Style	Brazilian MBA	Brazilian Worker	Foreign	
1. Participative	28% →	16%	33% →	30%
2. Paternalist	19% →	32%	10% →	20%
3. Authoritative	39% →	42%	21% →	22%
Styles 2+3	58% →	74%	31% →	42%

SOURCE ILB-Leadership Institute of Brazil, 2003.

(CCL) involved 20 different leadership representatives from Chile, Colombia, Mexico, Brazil and the United States. The discussion identified the main leadership challenges faced by leaders and organizations; the following summary presents the outstanding challenges that emerged at the session:

- aversion to change;
- narrow concept of leadership (transactional);
- don't know how to lead, to teach leadership;
- history of leaders who brought disappointment;
- ethical leadership: corruption;
- talent: pipeline, retention of expatriates;
- nepotism: family-owned businesses;
- socialist country: workers have rights;
- public/private collaboration to address intractable problems.

These results present both challenges that are generally widespread, and ones that are particular to the situation the region is currently facing (especially some of the later ones on the list). Nevertheless, the various studies give evidence of a slow transition towards a leadership style that clearly aims to embrace collaboration.

Emerging dimensions

Leaders are responsible for configuring the various elements of their organizations in a way that will generate the proper response to the many environmental demands. The global issues related to change management and the demands for innovation have created specific requirements in the modern leadership profile. As innovation is conceived as a process that thrives on multiple, diverse, independent and rapid experimentation, it requires Latin American leaders to identify within their companies' talent base and experience a particular set of capabilities (a task that at times may run counter to their cultural tendencies). The emerging demands for a more collaborative leadership style conceive the leader as a think-tank opener, creativity activator, opportunity explorer, change agent and creator of environments where innovation can flourish. According to Silverthorne, the key emphasis is on the basic construct of leaders as responsible for opening spaces for 'conversations about ideas across the organization', and to 'focus on rewarding and recognizing good creative work' (Silverthorne, 2002).

Dr William Guilory, from the organization *International Inventions*, promotes the development and adoption of a creative-adaptive mind for future leadership. He believes that the business environment will be dominated by the integration of knowledge, people and cooperation. Hamel, as cited by Kendall, believes that in the current era, structural, intellectual and financial resources need to be continuously reconfigured, re-launched and redirected to create new wealth. He also believes that for this to occur, organizations must build three types of capital: imaginative capital, venture capital and relational capital. These catalysts for wealth creation are becoming a mechanism to protect organizations against the risk of becoming irrelevant in a discontinuous world. The good news is that the interwoven fibres of Latin American culture have great potential to develop the three types of capital. For example, in relation to imaginative capital, Latin Americans are used to navigating turbulent, complex and at times dangerous work environments in such a way that some global corporations are coming more and more to value the intrinsic capacity of Latin Americans to cope with such demands. Innovation occurs in a failure-tolerant environment that values and accommodates constructive conflict; it is easy to recognize this environment as being exactly the one that most Latin Americans are used to navigating. The many and dramatic realities of the region have turned Latin American leaders into change experts. However, although the fit between the demands of the present era and Latin America's potential to cope with them gives hope, the path to the future is still uncertain. A shift into a new leadership reality requires a rethinking of the nature and schemes of perception in which the leader–follower interaction occurs.

An enabling context

Leaders are responsible for opening spaces for ideas-generation in the organization. Von Krogh and colleagues refer to this as 'an enabling context or Ba' (Von Krogh, Ichijo and Nonaka, 2000). The concept of 'Ba' comes from a Japanese term that refers to the idea of an organizational context, whether physical, virtual, mental or, more likely, a mix of the three. To create an enabling environment that fosters creativity and a sense of meaning requires the harmonization of many aspects, both tangible and intangible. That is why it is important to bring together organizational elements related to the structural, relational and motivational design for that purpose. The challenge is to create an environment that is as inclusive as possible. Allowing followers to participate in change-related decisions, including them in the design of that change and its implementation will make them feel part of the organization/project; and although their responsibilities will increase, they will be in a better position to cope with them. In this sense, the leader's role includes enabling adequate exchanges among people: designing and maintaining appropriate and comfortable offices, fostering initiatives that may ease conversations in hallways, assigning mentors, involving followers in experimentation events, and rewarding and recognizing good work and creativity, among other initiatives. In light of such challenges, some initiatives are evidently central to the processes that are taking place in the Latin American context:

- *The coaching philosophy* interwoven with the leadership essence epitomizes many of the key elements crucial to the transition towards a more collaborative interaction between leaders and followers in Latin America. Coaching is conceived as a process of establishing conversational partnerships that enable, clarify, motivate, engage and support people to fulfil their goals and purpose. Developing an open and transformative environment within organizations determines how adequately they will be able to face change and new ways of life. Cultural essentials (such as belief systems and values) need to be explored and addressed through engaging, probing and inspiring conversations led by people who know how to do it. Professional coach training has found some difficulty (mainly due to cultural norms) in establishing itself among executives, CEOs and leaders in the corporate world in Latin America. Perhaps one of the key factors is the collectivist approach to organizational life in the region. This creates an organizational sense of group commitment that makes people unwilling to talk openly about their peers or bosses, as they also function within the same sphere of influence. Developing a coaching culture within organizations can help leaders create a conversational environment, especially as it relates to the collective increase of consciousness about issues that relates to sustainability, innovation, flexibility and social impact.

- *Regulations that help to de-regulate:* Good intentions do not, alone, lead to the establishment of a collaborative environment. A commitment from the organizational leadership to formally develop a cross-functional code of empowerment is needed. Norms, rules and procedures are seen as necessary components of corporate systems and culture; however, if the leadership does not follow through on measures to revitalize these elements, or if opposite values are manifest in the leadership style in a way that emphasizes supervisory demands, this can end up by debilitating any organizational initiatives. The emerging leadership paradigm that rethinks how regulatory schemes are expressed can be see in the following organizational example. Ricardo Semler, Director of Semco, a manufacturing conglomerate of companies that just a few years ago became one of the fastest-growing in Brazil, has transformed his company from an autocratic organization to one where employees run the operation – they wear what they want, choose their own bosses, and come and go as they please. Some theorists have felt that Semler may have taken the doctrine of employee involvement to ridiculous extremes; it has faced overwhelming obstacles. His unusual approach to teamwork initially engendered a lot of enthusiasm yet this scheme is still to prove its results and its capacity to function within the Brazilian culture in general. It was after a health breakdown, attributed to work exhaustion when he was 25 years old, that he considered redefining his approach to organizational life. After that experience, he decided to remake the company into a true democracy: a place run on trust and freedom, not fear. During the 1980s, Semler made Semco a laboratory for unusual but successful management practices as the company became a very progressive and democratic workplace. All regulations were replaced with the rule of common sense, a rule that paves the way to rethink how empowerment takes place.

- *A transformational set of values:* A values system coherently furnished has the power to give new meaning to the concept of teamwork. Creating a more collaborative environment requires a values system on which it can be based. That system may comprise such qualities as tolerance, common sense, respect and shared decision making. Organizations that encourage employees to systematically reflect on such values have the potential to turn awareness into an advantage as they raise and align the collective conscience to new grounds. Purposefully exploring the individual, group and organization meaning of each value can transform the way people think about others, share the organizational life and take decisions together. Bravo and Piñango refer to various cases of organizations that dared to change, to think differently and give rise to 'unique organizational practices, and even curiosity'. An interesting case that reflects creative collaboration is SofOS, an organization that embraced participatory decision making and emerged victorious through it. According to Bravo and Piñango (2008), 'during the economic crisis generated by the strike of 2002, faced with the dilemma of closing or laying off staff, SofOS, a company committed to information technology, chose to analyse the problem with the employees and came up with a scheme to reduce wages that allowed everyone to keep their jobs. In this way workers and their families retained reasonable security and the company kept its specialized knowledge personnel, while winning the commitment of its employees.' SofOS responded favourably in a challenging time, and was able to demonstrate an underlying set of values that eased collaboration.

- *Physical environment:* An interesting organizational example of the way architecture and design make a difference in the way people feel and perform at work is shown in the case of Ciudad Banesco (Banesco City) in Venezuela. Although most people might think the name refers to a city per se, it actually relates to a bank building-complex that claims to be a kind of a 'city', mainly because of its aim of incorporating many of the necessary benefits that characterize a good city. Banesco is a bank in Caracas, Venezuela; its state-of-the art and progressive building has become an exemplar in many senses, and even received an annual construction prize in 2004. The building occupied the abandoned facilities of a Sears store, becoming the biggest bank office in Latin America. Covering 64,000 m², it was designed to be able to hold all the office workers in Caracas (nearly 3,500 people by then). But the size is matched by various features that help make it part of the 21st century's global paradigm. It is highly ecological and uses modular offices across all the floors in an effort to minimize physical barriers and facilitate cross-functional collaboration. Also, it has food courts, a gym, auditoriums, and parking space for all workers, with an obvious aim of improving working conditions and of fostering a harmonious way of life among workers. The design integrates organizational schemes in a way that is not common in other organizations and facilitates a wealth of creative interactions that may be expected to lead to a more productive organization.

The image of 'the boss' is not enough to get workers to develop commitment, loyalty and identification with the work and organization. The pattern of the traditional authoritarian leader in the Latin American organizational realm doesn't seem to be working any more. Forward-looking leaders in the region are developing the ability to express their power responsibly through the exercise of leadership. This expression involves: the ability to facilitate and assist the process of empowering the organization's talent-base; the ability to share leadership that promotes participation of the other actors involved in its decision-making and problem-solving endeavours; and the intention to develop a culture that encourages and promotes a leadership style characterized by constructive engagement, reconciliation of common interests and focus on results; and an exemplary environment where ethics, consistency, respect for others, responsibility, contribution and service are modelled, recognized and rewarded.

References

Bravo, O and Piñango, R (2008) Organizaciones que se atreven a desafinar, *Debates IESA*, 8 (4), p 88

Celis, MT y Hernandez, MY (1999) El comportamiento organizacional. Unenfoque teóricópuáctico en el contexbo venezolano. Bárbula, Venezuela

Gouillory, WA (2007) 'The future perfect organization – leadership for the twenty-first century: part 2', *Industrial and Commercial Training*, 39 (2), pp 91–97

Kendall, S (2001) How Things Change: Five top gurus' views on innovation principles and practices, *CIO Magazine* (retrived on 25 February 2007 from www.cio.com/article/3045515_top_Guues_Talk_Innovation)

Marquardt, MJ and Berger, NO (2000) *Global Leaders for the 21st Century*, State University of New York Press, Albany, NY

Márquez, L and De Avellán, M (2008) ¿Cómo lidera el gerente Venezolano? *El Universal-Venezuela* [Online] www.eud.com (accessed 22 April 2008)

McIntosh, TA and Irving, JA (2010) Evaluating the Instrumento de Contribución al Liderazgo de Siervo (ICLS) for reliability in Latin America, *Journal of Virtues & Leadership*, 1 (1), pp 30–49

Pereira, O (2011) Dealing with development challenges: cultural perspectives and personal experiences in Brazil, panel presentation at the International Conference of the International Leadership Association (ILA), London, 7 October 2011

Santana, L (2011) Latin American leadership: one region with a world of opportunities, panel presentation at the International Conference of the International Leadership Association (ILA), London, 7 October 2011

Silverthorne, S (2002) *Time Pressure and Creativity: Why time is not on your side*, Harvard Business School Publishing/Working Knowledge [Online] http://hbswk.hbs.edu/item/3030.html (accessed 18 January 2007)

Von Krogh, G, Ichijo, K and Nonaka, I (2000) *Enabling Knowledge Creation: How to unlock the mystery of tacit knowledge and release the power of innovation*, Oxford University Press, Oxford

Long civilization, changing times and school leadership in China

08

Based on the practice of Chinese school principals in recent decades

JIACHENG LI

A great age calls for and develops great leaders. Chinese school principals are part of this leadership. They have developed new practices in dramatically changing times, building on a long history of civilization, and they are leading Chinese schools into a new era. This is a difficult task and a great calling, but Chinese principals have accepted the challenges and set themselves to answer it.

This chapter focuses on Chinese principals' leadership, to illustrate the new meaning of leadership arising from their practice. The data comes from the past three decades of Chinese school leadership development, and is especially based on the *New Basic Education Project* (NBEP) conducted by principals, teachers and professors from 1994. During 1994–99, five Shanghai schools and one university were involved in it; from 1999 to 2004, nearly 20 professors and doctoral graduate students, 2,000 teachers and principals, 56 schools and five districts (Minhang, Shanghai; Chongmin, Shanghai; Nanan, Fujian; Tianhe, Guangzhou, Guangdong; Linzi, Zibo, Shandong) participated; from 2004 to 2009, 10 schools, 976 teachers, 13,000 students, three districts (Minhang, Shanghai; Changzhou, Jiangsu; Putuo, Shanghai) and over 17 professors participated (Ye, 1999, 2004, 2009; Ye and Li, 2010). The NBEP has continued since 2009, and some principals and schools, including the author, have been in the programme for over 13 years.

A demanding calling

Great changes have taken place since the last century in China, especially from the 1980s. From the ecological point of view, it has been a period of rapid change at many levels, in which difficulties have converged and new dimensions have developed (Bronfenbrenner, 1979; Ye, 2006). The ecology of schooling is completely different from what it was in the past and from the Western pattern. Any principal has to 'look outward toward the larger society and inward toward the operation of the organization itself' (Guthrie and Schuermann, 2010: 27).

Though many external elements influence school leadership, a school is still an independent system with its own internal ecology. It must be viewed as a super-complex system dealing with the complexity of human beings, of the organization, of the process, and of the interaction between the school and the society. Definitely, school leadership matters.

In the past 30 years, great economic and political advances have been achieved while cultural and social problems increased rapidly, and the new educational system has been coming into being. Under such conditions, Chinese principals are facing a series of challenges:

- From where to where?
- How to achieve it?
- By whom?
- What does the leadership reform mean for the principals?

FIGURE 8.1 Leadership, tradition and change

In the past, it was not difficult to answer such questions: a school was managed by the principal under the authority of the government; the main goal of management was to maintain discipline and high grades; school leadership was assessed by the government; the principal was always regarded as an official, and didn't have to be trained to be professional, though he or she was always a good teacher; management theories based on the practice of business management were always popular in schools, as if the school was no different from a factory or corporation.

But now, times are changing dramatically and will continue changing, just as the British writer Hilarie Owen said (2007: 97):

> Our world is made up of interconnected energy and this is the new paradigm for leadership. Management is about control and is based on the Cartesian mindset of seeing organizations including schools as machines; leadership is about the relationship between a leader and others, and how they interconnect to bring about change. The internet and globalization are both showing the interconnectiveness of our world today. Management is about adapting to the existing context. Leadership is about creating the context.

Yes, this is the time for Chinese principals to take school leadership reform as a demanding task and calling.

The new meaning of school leadership

During the past 30 years, Chinese principals have developed school leadership, and fostered a theory of leadership with Chinese characteristics. We will discuss the four elements of this theory: it is value oriented and action based, and entails both relation-context and sphere-pursuit (as discussed below).

Value oriented

What should one do as a principal? This is the first question challenging school leaders. In a stable society, there is no urgent need to answer the

TABLE 8.1 Ecology of school leadership in China

Macrosystem	**Globalization**	➤ International organizations ➤ Interaction between countries ➤ Localism and globalism
	Science and technology	➤ Information technology ➤ Knowledge society
Exosystem	**Political**	➤ Democracy ➤ Decision making by scientific methods ➤ Government reform ➤ Balance and integration of public good and private good
	Economic	➤ New economy ➤ New working skills ➤ Job opportunity
	Societal	➤ One-child policy ➤ New generation of parents ➤ Family and community ➤ Social classes
	Cultural	➤ East and West ➤ Transformation and development of culture ➤ Value and life mode ➤ Sub-culture
Mesosystem	**Educational system**	➤ Educational quality and education system reform ➤ Autonomy and profession ➤ Support and accountability ➤ Curriculum reform
Microsystem	School leadership	➤ Principals ➤ Teachers ➤ Students ➤ Parents

FIGURE 8.2 The four elements of leadership with Chinese characteristics

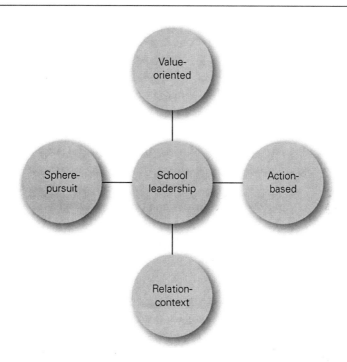

question; but in changing times with shifting values, it is becoming more important to set one's mind to answer it (Collins, 2001; Ye, 2006; Li, 2006a).

The value of schooling comes first, the value of leadership comes second. A principal is responsible for every aspect of a school that may be involved with thousands of families, for the lives and careers of the students and teachers, and for serving the society around it. The leadership is not of a *factory*, but of a *school*. The first essential is to clarify the value of schooling, and only then to consider the leadership.

Why is that? In the past, it was common to apply the management theory of a factory or corporation to schools. But what is unique to school leadership? What is the difference between the two organizations? Now, more and more principals ask the question: If I am the principal of the school then, what is the purpose of school leadership? Test scores? Discipline? The answer is: the well-being of students and teachers (Ye, 1999; Morin, 2004; Li, 2006a).

First, let all students develop actively and healthily in school

The school life matters (Dewey, 1916; Jackson, 1968; Jackson, Boostrom and Hansen 1998; Ye, 2006). The value of schooling for children lies not only in achieving academic success, but also in developing their emotional and social sides, and in fulfilling their potential. In one sentence, let the children learn to be, not to be disciplined or ruled (International Commission on the Development of Education, 1972; Ye, 2006).

But this was not easy to do in the old system. Students were mostly silent in school, seeking answers in books, and studying for test scores by memorizing knowledge. Though some students volunteered to answer questions, they had little chance to speak out or engage in dialogue because they had little free time of their own, few diverse and open spaces to learn, and limited opportunities to ask, plan, organize or assess their learning by themselves. Quite a few high school students had negative perceptions of learning in the classroom (Li, 2010), as shown in Table 8.2.

Another survey (Tables 8.3 and 8.4, Figures 8.3 and 8.4) revealed more about the perceptions among pre-college students about the value of learning.

In this context, Chinese principals need to clarify their values about schooling: What is it for? What objectives should it achieve? In recent decades, the focus has changed from discipline to the active and healthy development of students based on the notion of student as an active learner in his/her own life (Bransford, Brown and Cocking, 2000; Sawyer, 2006; Darling-Hammond et al, 2008; Dumont, Istance and Benavides, 2010; Ye, 1997; Ye, Jinchu, 2006). For example, Shanghai Yucai High School sets 'self-management, self-learning and self-exercise' as the mission of schooling. The principal of Beijing Shiyi High School criticized the test-oriented approach to schooling and worked to transform the school into an 'educative' and 'research-based' high school (Li Jinchu, 2006). Middle and elementary schools have focused strongly on the happiness of learning and the whole life of students since the 1980s.

In contrast to some Western countries, Chinese principals have developed a number of new educational areas in schooling: for example, the classroom community at class level and what I call student-comprehensive-development at school level, meaning the experience of learning that is based on the life of the student. For Chinese principals, the *class* is not only a place for the teacher to conduct instruction, but also a community for students, in which they can decorate the classroom, make rules and decisions, and socialize with each other. At school level, there are various clubs, student government bodies,

TABLE 8.2 High school students' learning in the classroom

	Strongly Disagree	Disagree	Uncertain	Agree	Strongly Agree	Average	Standard Deviation
Students respond actively to the questions given by the teacher	10.8%	28.8%	25.8%	24.2%	10.4%	2.95	1.173
Students always have opportunities to ask questions or give comments	21.0%	37.8%	21.2%	14.3%	5.7%	2.46	1.138
Every student can be involved in the discussion or other learning activities	13.7%	30.5%	28.6%	18.8%	8.4%	2.78	1.152
It is easy to learn in groups	16.8%	33.3%	26.3%	16.7%	6.9%	2.64	1.148
Students always conduct collaborate-learning or inquiring by groups	15.7%	31.0%	25.1%	19.6%	8.7%	2.74	1.190
Students listen to each other during the discussion	22.0%	40.4%	24.6%	9.3%	3.7%	2.32	1.033
Students always share their thoughts and feelings	22.8%	37.3%	25.3%	9.5%	5.1%	2.37	1.088

SOURCE Survey of students from January to December 2008 in 11 Provinces and 96 High Schools (N=23,698).

TABLE 8.3 Why do you want to be a college student?

A	To get a good job	66.70%
B	To improve my qualifications	18.20%
C	For my parents	5.20%
D	Never thought about this; other people do it so I do the same	5.40%
E	Other	4.60%

TABLE 8.4 How do you prepare for college?

A	I focus on test scores, but have not thought about a particular college or subject	44.50%
B	I know which college I want to attend, but have not thought about a particular subject or research area	21.10%
C	I know which subject I want to study, but have not thought about a particular college	9.70%
D	I have decided on a college and subject, but have not thought about my long-term aims	12.00%
E	I have decided on a college and subject, and am clear about my long-term aims	9.70%
F	Other	3.00%

field trips and many celebrations that are also educating moments and places. Many Chinese schools have a specific office, the 'student-comprehensive-development office', to help teachers and students. The value of this is also pointed out by John Dewey: 'It [provides] a chance to be a miniature community, and embryonic society' (Dewey, 1959: 18). One theorist has said that 'citizenship is actually learned in and through the processes and practices that make up the everyday lives of children, young people and adults' (Biesta, 2011: 1). In Chinese schools, the contents and process of classroom-community-development and student-comprehensive-development are quite different from formal instruction by teachers in class. They include:

FIGURE 8.3 Why do you want to be a college student?

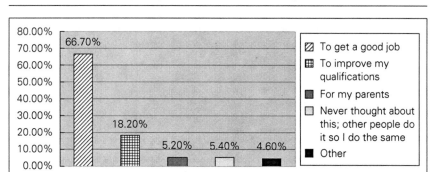

FIGURE 8.4 How do you prepare for college?

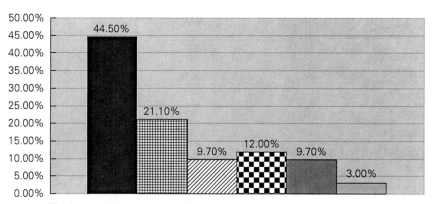

SOURCE Survey of Grade 12 students from December 2005 to February 2006, in 21 high schools in Shanghai, (N=4,170).

- organizing a group, formal or informal, long or short term;
- group study and service, self-management, investigating and presenting, competing and cooperating with other groups;
- developing a class culture (rules, targets and cultural symbols);
- electing classroom leaders and assessing leaders in class;
- planning and attending class meetings (once a week or more, of different kinds and depth of engagement);
- planning and carrying out grade-level or school-level activities (graduation ceremonies, science fairs, arts fairs, athletic meetings, field trips and others), and helping peers in school (eg a 'big-hand in small-hand' programme);[1]
- operating clubs and student council or committee;
- developing in partnership with families and the community;
- being involved in discussing and acting on social issues.

Second, let teachers enjoy professional dignity and happiness

Teachers' qualifications are crucial for good schooling. But what about the quality of teachers' lives? If teachers are not creatively involved in their work, that will affect the students seriously, and ultimately will have a deep influence on the teacher too (Jackson, 1992; Ye, 1997).

Over the past 30 years, Chinese principals have focused on this aspect of school life:

- *Teachers' self-awareness of life*: getting teachers to balance the relationship between education and their own lives, and to use the wisdom and creativity they have rather than working and living passively and negatively. Principals should respect the innovation and autonomy of teachers, foster their professionalism and support their work.

- *Developing research-based practice*: the personal qualities and professional standards of teachers are both promoted in everyday teaching and classroom life, in individual learning or group communication and interaction, and in interaction with students and colleagues. Principals should encourage the teachers to turn daily life into research-based practice, and lead such reforms in school.

- *Living in the ecology of teacher groups*: lesson-preparation groups, teaching and research groups, grade groups and other organizations can enhance group communication, cooperation and mutual learning. Principals should develop such groups or sub-organizations in school, and ensure that they benefit the development of teachers.

Take Xunyang Road Elementary School as an example. Teachers there have many opportunities to discuss their work and get feedback from others, and have more opportunities to fulfil their strengths and achieve success. In 2009, four teachers of the second grade conducted formal research-based class teaching 32 times, working in cooperation with other teachers; on average every teacher observed 14 of these presentations.[2] For example, besides teaching her own grade-group, Mrs Haijun Wu made more than 10 presentations to all the Chinese literature teachers of the school. All these contributed to the development of teachers, and the success and happiness of their school life.

Pursuing new schooling or a new school

The modern school in China has been developed only in the last 100 years – China has a long history of education, but a short one of schooling. What does the ideal school look like today? There are no models or examples for Chinese principals, but they have to transform the old pattern of schooling to a new one; this is the goal of school leadership – to develop a *new* school (Wu and Li, 2007). How can Chinese principals achieve this?

It is really challenging. Ernest Boyer tried to imagine a *basic school;* as he said:

> An effective school connects people, to create *community.* An effective school connects the curriculum, to achieve *coherence.* An effective school connects classrooms and resources, to enrich the learning *climate.* And an effective school connects learning to life, to build *character* (Boyer, 1995: 8).

Such ideas and many kinds of theories, policies and school leadership movements have come on the scene, but some educationalists are still puzzled that so little has been achieved, and have tried to explain why this is so (Rose, 2009; Ravitch, 2010; Labaree, 2010).

Chinese principals are doing their best, basing their work both on a long history of civilization and on changing times. Principals in the NBEP are trying to apply a new framework to leadership. To them, the *new school* concept means: enhancing value, decentralizing the work, opening the structure, being interactive in process and internalizing the motivation of learners (Ye, 2004, 2006). The Seven-flower Elementary School of Shanghai has tried to develop a school culture of beauty, harmony and happiness. In teaching, community relations and all aspects of its activities, the aim is to make schooling a richly rewarding experience for all concerned. After three years' endeavour, the principal and teachers are making great strides towards turning this concept from a blueprint into a reality. Meanwhile, the Jianping High School in Shanghai is working on school reforms that will shift the focus from one of maintaining the school's resources to *institutional* development, which in turn will lead on to *cultural* development. There are many similar cases of such developments in China, with *new schools* emphasizing the *value of schooling*, suited to *each individual* school, and developed with *professional autonomy*.

Through these efforts, the framework of a *new school* ideal is emerging. It includes:

- a vision for the school;
- a culture for the school;
- school institutions;
- a school-based curriculum;
- effective teaching;
- development of classroom-communities and development of all aspects of students lives;
- quality teachers;
- collaboration with families and communities.

Action-based leadership

Some have criticized educationalists in the past for confusing 'moral problems' with 'intellectual problems', and argued that the true focus of education should be on 'deciding what it should do', and on 'acting' or 'do' that (Null and Ravitch, 2006). In China, 'knowing' and 'doing' are connected, even integrated. We believe that knowledge comes from practice, and we also focus on what we do for the well-being of students and the community.

Derived from such a background, Chinese school leadership is action-based. As Owen (2007: 4–5) so rightly said:

> Leadership is not a job title; it is both a state of being and a state of doing. The Being state has to involve authenticity, integrity, courage and self-knowledge; the Doing state has to involve challenging what is, taking responsibility and action, taking people with you and knowing that even if you don't know what may be at the end of it, you know it is the right path to take.

The action cycle

The work of a principal is hard, and sometimes confusing. This can easily lead to short-term views and actions. To counter this, some theorists have put forward the notion of the *inquiry–action cycle* (Militello, Rallis and Goldring, 2009), outlined in Figure 8.5 and discussed below. Recognizing the long-term requirements of schooling and school leadership, Chinese principals are trying to foster such an action cycle.

FIGURE 8.5 The inquiry–action cycle

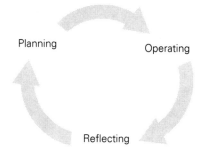

Planning

Operating

Reflecting

Planning

In the past, under the bureaucratic and hierarchical system governing education, Chinese principals used to *manage* their schools along lines laid down by government officials. Since the end of the 20th century, however, the school-planning movement has helped produce a major transformation in school leadership (Davies, 2009; Guthrie and Schuermann, 2010; Darling-Hammond et al, 2010).

First, planning is recognized as an essential part of school leadership. An old Chinese saying goes: *No planning, No achieving*. School leadership is a very complex task, one that must take account of a long period that will critically influence all the pupils, teachers and parents; it is dangerous to jump into such a task without proper preparation. Good planning is a vital tool to allow the principal and staff to clarify the values and objectives – and the challenges – of the process.

Second, the planning process is a leadership process. In many cities and provinces, principals spend more than six months on planning new school developments before engaging in the three-year or five-year cycle. The planning is undertaken by the principal, teachers, parents, students and various experts; it involves much investigation, discussion and re-framing, and it must be approved by the committee of all teachers. In such a process, the principal can identify problems, discuss approaches with teachers and parents, get assistance from experts, clarify the values, inspire the staff, and move the school into a well-planned cycle of activity.

Third, the planning process is a process of development. Teachers, parents and students are involved in the planning, and so acquire a clear understanding of how the school aims to develop, and especially of their responsibility for (and need of) individual development. More and more elements emerge during the process, and they will affect the school's development. Leaders in different areas of schooling will each take responsibility for the development of one specific field, such as teaching or school resources; in so doing, they will improve their planning abilities, including the skills of collaborating and problem-solving. In the planning process, teachers are always asked to make individual personal development plans for a three-year or five-year period. All of these elements lead to the development of the teachers, staff and the school.

Operating

Some theorists may criticize the planning of school reforms and argue that the blueprint does not always matter. In the view of Chinese principals, however, success depends on action during and after the process of planning. In fact, planning is central to the whole process of school development and leadership.

Operating is the responsibility of everyone in school, and the planning process clarifies the responsibilities of every staff member. During the three-year or five-year development period, teachers and principals must demonstrate through their actions that they are striving to achieve the objectives they have set themselves. Everyone takes on responsibilities for some aspect of operations, such as changing the teaching style, enhancing collaboration with parents, conducting the clubs, bringing new technologies into teaching, and so on.

To operate successfully, all those involved must coordinate their actions. In the daily life of the school, the principal and his/her colleagues should be fully aware of everyone and every area. In school meetings, which take place at least once a week for executive councils and once a month for all teachers, the principal will give feedback, solve problems, discuss progress with teachers and make new decisions. The box below shows an example of an executive council meeting.

At executive councils, the directors of various departments summarize the work of the last week, and raise various issues. Then, the principal highlights some areas of work, points out shortfalls if necessary, and assigns work for the next week.

After the summer holidays in 2007, the school participated in the *New Basic Education Project*. The first reform topic for the executive council was a *case analysis*. On the executive council, directors reported on their work of the last week and commented on achievements and problems. After that, the principal outlined the case and conducted an in-depth analysis together with the other council members.

This pattern of *case analysis* was used for more than a year. At the end of that time, the arrival of more than 700 teachers and students from another primary school led to new challenges and complexity. From then on, before the council met the directors would provide papers on particular topics, based on current research, and everyone made full preparation. On the council, every director could speak out freely, and put forward constructive suggestions for his/her own or other departments. After that, everyone would give some comments and analysis on the case.

After November 2009, the executive council meetings changed once again, to a style that the staff call *deep talks*. The council now meet every two weeks, rather than a weekly as in the past, and select for discussion core issues such as school development planning, department plans and so on. Rather than dealing with a range of disparate points, the executive council focuses on ways to promote school reform. This has enhanced the quality of discussions, reflection and planning; every director participates in the council, raising problems and contributing ideas, expressing his/her views, and learning from the others.

Source: Dongfang Elementary School, Changzhou City, 2010.

To operate well requires development to be consistent, and the operations themselves become a problem-solving process too. The school leader must encourage the staff, give them ample support, and above all, be a model to them. This is always recognized as the most important aspect of instructional leadership for principals. Many Chinese principals put a great deal of time into teaching, including discussing teaching plans, observing what happens in the classroom and reviewing lessons with the teacher after the class. Chinese teachers collaborate with and learn from each other easily and effectively. In one elementary school, teachers of the same subject and grade came together to perform what they *called three-phases of teaching and two-cycles of reflection*; this approach, which may last several days for one topic, has benefited all those involved (see Figure 8.6).

FIGURE 8.6 Three-phases of teaching and two-cycles of reflection

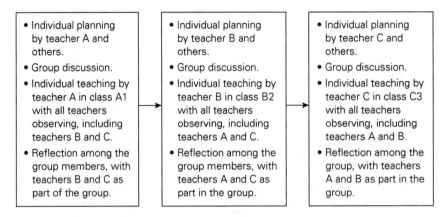

- Individual planning by teacher A and others.
- Group discussion.
- Individual teaching by teacher A in class A1 with all teachers observing, including teachers B and C.
- Reflection among the group members, with teachers B and C as part of the group.

- Individual planning by teacher B and others.
- Group discussion.
- Individual teaching by teacher B in class B2 with all teachers observing, including teachers A and C.
- Reflection among the group members, with teachers A and C as part in the group.

- Individual planning by teacher C and others.
- Group discussion.
- Individual teaching by teacher C in class C3 with all teachers observing, including teachers A and B.
- Reflection among the group, with teachers A and B as part in the group.

SOURCE Xunyang Road Elementary School of Shanghai, 2004.

Reflecting

School leadership is an endless process, and can feel like rebuilding a plane while keeping it in the air, loaded with passengers. It is demanding for the principals and the leadership-group members, and there may seem little time to reflect on the school development, but such reflection is a valuable way to learn and develop. Opportunities include:

- *End of term/year-reflection.* After each term or year of work, every Chinese principal reflects on the work, by discussing with colleagues, investigating various aspects of school life and drawing conclusions. Then, he or she gives a full report to all the staff, and to the district.

- *Daily reflection.* The principal has many opportunities to observe lessons, talk with students and parents, visit other schools or be visited by other teachers, and discuss progress with the leadership-group members. So he or she is always in the process of reflecting. This is one of the elements of decision making, and a creative force for the development of both the school and leadership.

- *Reflecting on role models.* Since the last decade of the 20th century, there has been an ever increasing focus on the reflecting abilities of teachers. Teaching is a demanding calling for all the members of the school. In order to be a leader of a studying-organization, and to develop the teachers, the principal must serve as a model and accept his/her responsibility to educate others.

With globalization and the development of Chinese schooling, principals have more opportunities to observe and communicate with others, which will encourage valuable habits of reflection. In this way, the school leadership can evolve into an open and dynamic system.

Complex thinking

Our ways of thinking will influence, sometimes decisively, our action, and a principal must have, or develop, a quality 'thinking-mode' (Fullan, 1993, 1999, 2005; Wagner et al, 2006; Li, 2008). In Chinese culture, some thinking-modes are always valued, such as dialectical-thinking, developmental-thinking and systematic-thinking. Nowadays, a range of issues are challenging Chinese principals:

- the environment and the internal dynamics of the school, such as the quality of parents, support in the neighbourhood, government financial support, etc;
- building a vision, and the difficult processes involved in bringing it to life, such as how to motivate all teachers, how to deal with day-to-day life, how to enhance their reflecting ability;
- the school as a whole and its different parts, dealing with lack of balance among the different subjects, the varied focus and support needed in different areas, ensuring coherence among different elements, the wholeness of the school development, etc.

These challenges are related to the thinking-mode of the principal. The efforts of Chinese principals are rewarding, and they have achieved some of their success by relating their work to Chinese culture and the changing age.

You-and-I thinking

School reform deserves great public support, but this is a period of rapid upheaval, and among its greatest challenges is the systematic reform of education. Principals are facing real difficulties, such as the demands of autonomous development, the problems of engaging parents, and the quality of teachers. Can we wait for all the external elements to change? We could, but we should not, for the sake of today's children. In Chinese culture, we appreciate our responsibility for the individual, family and the nation, and this is a firm basis for positive thinking among principals.

This is not the time for delay. Principals themselves have to take the lead, starting from today. Each must declare *I am part of the environment*, because what school principals have done and are doing is crucial for the whole education and social system. Let each declare *I am a force*, because in such a complex, changing age everyone may be a force for change. If the principal declares and believes that *I am the leader of this micro-system*, then he or she can relate dynamically to others (relate *you* and *I*), and can think in an '*I-way*', with a more positive attitude and a more productive style.

Possibility and real-life thinking

How can one achieve a *new school*? How does one lead a *changing* school? There is little experience to draw upon; there is almost no one who can teach the principals how to do these things. Hence, Chinese principals have great ideas, but don't always know how to turn them into reality.

In real life, Chinese principals are trying to relate *theory* to *practice*, so that they can clarify their thinking, identify the goals, and apply the theories in their own leadership practice. At the same time, they are trying to develop their own theory from their own practice. This is achieved by *learning and leading by doing*. Through doing, principals can test ideas, and can arrive at new visions of what is possible. This kind of thinking makes principals think more positively and act more bravely. Principals also realize the importance of *learning from the past and the outside world*. The modern school system was only established within the last century, and there have been many great principals, such as Xingzhi Tao, Boling Zhang and Lipei Duan, who created a new era for Chinese education. In addition to this, we have a history of thousands of years of education, an almost unimaginable wealth accumulated by a long civilization. On the other hand, with the shrinking of the world, Chinese principals have more opportunities to learn from colleagues around the world. All of these elements are changing the principals' thinking mode.

One-and-more thinking

To evolve a systematic approach to education is one of the greatest tasks for Chinese principals today. Due to the short history of schooling and school leadership, the rapid development of our education system, and the changing times in China, some principals have focused on developing 'one outstanding programme': the 'specialist school'. This is valuable, but it is not everything. In China, a range of problems will influence the development of the whole school; one of the most difficult of these is that the organization may focus only on one subject, one activity, one teacher or one moment.

As the leadership role model for the school, the principal should lead reform of the whole system; all its aspects are interrelated and influence each other. Hence, the principal must be a systematic leader, and must think '*more than one*', finding and fostering the *more in one*.

This mode of thinking, so rich and rewarding, is becoming fundamental to the lives of Chinese principals.

Innovation

The process of leadership is one of school reform and of developing new schooling – it is about creating new possibilities. Principals must foster innovation, identify its potentialities, drive it through and establish it in the daily life of the new school. Decades of endeavours have contributed to ever increasing innovation in Chinese schooling.

The first and the foremost aspect of this is *new teaching and learning*. 'Meaningful educational changes must ultimately occur in classrooms' (Militello, Rallis and Goldring, 2009). Labaree points out that changing the way teachers teach in their individual classrooms has been much more challenging; and changing how and what students learn in those classrooms has proven to be the most daunting of all reform aims (Labaree, 2010). Maybe this is the reason for the importance of instructional leadership or learning-centred leadership (Southworth, 2009; Darling-Hammond et al, 2010; Murphy et al, 2006).

In Chinese schools, principals conduct teaching and learning-centred leadership in many ways:

- classroom visits;
- discussion of lesson plans;
- discussion of teaching after class;
- critical friends' groups;
- open courses/classes;
- case studies;
- assessment of teaching by school and government;
- visiting other schools together with their teachers;
- being involved in academic research projects.

We can take a framework of teaching assessment as an example that can represent the shared vision of good teaching (Bransford, Brown and Cocking, 2000; Donovan and Bransford, 2005; Wagner et al, 2006; Darling-Hammond et al, 2008). Principals in Shanghai and Jiangsu who are involved in the NBEP use the tools shown in Tables 8.5 and 8.6 to assess the learning and teaching.

TABLE 8.5 Record of classroom observations

Year _____ Month _____ Day _____

School: _____ Grade: _____ Class: _____

Teachers: _____ Subject: _____

Textbook: _____ Lesson time: _____

Teaching methods: _____ Number of students: _____

Records of the number of cases of individual dialogue between the teacher and students (writing "正" in the corresponding box):

Door - - - - - - - - platform - - - - - - - - - window

	1	2	3	4	5	6	7	8	9	10	
1											1
2											2
3											3
4											4
5											5
6											6
7											7
8											8
9											9
10											10

1　2　3　4　5　6　7　8　9　10

Records of other forms of activities (writing "正" in the corresponding place):

1. Whole-class activities:
2. Everyone's independent activity:
3. Group activities:

Content number	Exchanging ideas	Operating	Discussing			
Two-students						
Four-students						
Six-students						
Free-grouping						

4. Continuity by row: _____
5. Continuity but not by row: _____
6. Individual student answers 5 questions posed to all students: _____

_____

7. Presentation to the whole class: Single: _____ Multiplayer: ___ Team: ___
8. Others:

* This table was produced in March 2001, and has been in use since September 2001.
SOURCE *New Basic Education Project*, September, 2001.

TABLE 8.6 Evaluation framework for teaching

1. Evaluation of teaching design

Item	Index	Score		
		A (1)	B (0.7)	C (0.5)
Teaching objects design	① Clarity and specificity of teaching objects			
	② Stating the level of students			
	③ Considering the possibilities of students development			
Teaching content design	① Focusing on the relation between subject content and real-world life			
	② Focusing on the flexibility and structure of content			
	③ Focusing on the educational value of the subject			
Teaching process design	① The type of activities of teacher and students			
	② The validity of activities			
	③ Flexibility of design			

2. Evaluation of teaching process

Item	Index	Score		
		A (1)	B (0.7)	C (0.5)
Routine activities	① Appropriateness of the pace			
	② Flexibility in combination of parts and whole			
	③ Interest level of activity form			

TABLE 8.6 *continued*

Importing openly	① Rational and openness			
	② Divergent and openness			
	③ Profound and openness			
Generation of resources	① Self-activity time of students, and validity of independent learning			
	② The variety of resources generation			
	③ The quality of resource generation			
Feedback	① Teacher's feedback in time			
	② Clarity and advancement of feedback			
	③ Sensitivity of new resources			
Generation in process	① The utilization of resource			
	② Ability to compare, analysis, comprehension and restructuring			
	③ Formation of further study programmes			
Interactive and deepening	① The degree of interactivity between students			
	② The quality of interactivity between students			
	③ The degree of interactivity between teachers and students			
Clarity of conclusion	① The clarity of conclusion and refining			
	② The length of content			
	③ Openness and practicality of homework			

TABLE 8.6 *continued*

3. Evaluation of teaching reflection

Item	Index	Score		
		A (1)	B (0.7)	C (0.5)
Self-evaluation	① Appropriateness of comprehensive evaluation			
	② Specificity of comprehensive evaluation			
	③ Clarity of self-consciousness			
Problems Reflection	① Appropriateness of problem attribution			
	② Clarity of retrospection			
	③ Depth of retrospection			
Reconstruction of teaching	① Possibility of promoting design			
	② Pertinence of promoting design			
	③ Promotion to higher levels			

SOURCE *New Basic Education Project*, September 2001.

Does this kind of leadership matter? Let's take a struggling middle school in the NBEP, Minhang No 4 Middle School in Shanghai, as an example. When the students enrolled in 2002, two tests of Chinese literature and mathematics were conducted by the district; when the same students graduated in 2006, there was another test for all schools in this district. The results are shown in Table 8.7.

Teaching and learning-centred leadership benefits the development of students and teachers. The teaching and learning go beyond the limits of subject-teaching or learning, and improve the well-being of the whole life of the school.

TABLE 8.7 Academic achievement of MNo 4 MS students

	Number of students		Pass rate in Chinese literature		Average score in Chinese literature		Pass rate in mathematics		Average score in mathematics	
	2002	2006	2002	2006	2002	2006	2002	2006	2002	2006
MNo 4MS	242	209	54.84	98.56	59.52	113.1	86	98.56	76.4	127.0
Minhang District	6,871	6,403	74.03	98.61	65.35	115.4	88.28	92.14	79.47	121.2

SOURCE Minhang No 4 Middle School of Shanghai, 2009.

The second innovation is new organizations and cultures. The new school must have a new structure, new departments and a new culture. In Chinese schools, the previous system of subdivisions has been revised, and new departments have been set up. These include:

- teaching departments;
- a department of student-comprehensive-development;
- research departments;
- a department for investigation, decision making and feedback;
- assessment and grading groups;
- teaching and researching groups;
- 'lab' of top teachers.[3]

The operating rules and responsibilities of different departments have been re-considered and renewed in many schools. For example, Huaping Elementary school in Shanghai spent more than a year on revising the school rules, by 'deleting', 'modifying', 'combining' and 'updating' them to develop a new school system.

The different groups or departments work in collaboration, taking responsibility for different areas, and learning from each other. Between them they engender learning, collaboration and a developing culture in schools. This is a way of life for teachers and principal, and this is just what *culture* means – a living-mode for human beings. Principals and teachers can instil such culture into the school spirit through painting the building, making speeches or writing articles.

The third innovation, and perhaps the most difficult and important one, is the self-renewal of teachers and principals. Through constant inquiry based on sound research, through reflecting on their work, and learning/renewing themselves in action, principals, teachers and pupils develop quickly. And in recent years more systematic support from the government has helped to accelerate this process.

The context of relationships

Leadership occurs not in isolation but in specific contexts; relationships are placing new demands on schools, but also make principals pivotal both in meeting those demands and in making the best use of the available resources (Southworth, 2009; Militello, Rallis and Goldring, 2009).

In Chinese culture, we view the individual as part of the group, we focus on the social networks of work and life, and we see leadership as a process that integrates many interacting forces. In an age of change, this culture shapes modern school leadership.

Interaction with teachers

Chinese principals are drawn from a pool of the best and most successful teachers, so they are highly experienced in the profession and familiar with the tasks teachers face. Labaree (2010) listed five levels of school reform: rhetoric, government, principals, teachers and students. If we view this through the lens of complex system theory, we may say it is more than a hierarchy or linear system; principals and teachers are vital for different elements, and they interact and affect each other. Chinese principals value the autonomy of teaching and the independence of teachers, and realize the importance of collaboration with them. In the process of leadership, the principal respects the teachers, discusses things with them and, more importantly, creates opportunities for them to fulfil their potential, not only as leaders and teachers but in other areas too. Such collaboration is a constant theme in the school's work, in the classroom, administration and school activities.

Interaction with leader-group members

In every school there is a group of leaders who support the principal, ranging from associate or assistant principals through heads of departments and middle-level or sub-group leaders. At one time Chinese principals were seen as *giant* figures, but more and more of them are realizing that individual power is not as effective as group power. Furthermore, principals have a responsibility to develop the leadership potential of group leaders. This has produced a pattern of distributed leadership, aimed at strategic development and at actively realizing the full strengths of a school (Rath and Conchie, 2008). Principals also emphasize informal communication with others, and help to solve problems beyond the school leadership with care. This too is part of Chinese culture: *we live together, we care for each other, and we help each other.*

Interaction with professors

Many different forces are contributing to the reform of Chinese school leadership, and among them is the work of theorists and academics. Some professors are eager to collaborate with principals, to put theory into practice and to develop new understanding from practice. For principals and teachers, this can provide a professional underpinning of great value to the school. Some theorists have defined the different kinds of partnership as *technical, technical/support, conceptual, transformative* and *emancipatory* (eg Willis, 2011). In China, however, principals, teachers and professors see the possibility of a new relationship: one of integration that provides mutual benefit for all as they move into the future. They set the school, school leadership and school reform as the common goals to achieve, aiming to build Chinese pedagogy, leadership and schools. This kind of collaboration can be found in Shanghai, Beijing, Hubei, Guangxi or Yunnan. In Shanghai, such cooperation between professors, principals and teachers has been going on for several decades, and a range of projects have been undertaken over the past 20 years. Principals there can invite professors to become involved in such processes as planning, classroom teaching, staff development and assessment (Ye, 2006; Yang, 2002; Wu, 2009).

Interaction with other schools

Principals and schools live in the real world, and must be closely involved with other schools. Decades ago, there was intense competition among schools on testing scores, resources and reputation. With the development of education and changes in fundamental views of schooling, however, there has been more collaboration and exchange of ideas. Principals and teachers visit other schools more often, and run research projects together; this has fostered a learning culture that has expanded beyond the district level and is now extending to inter-province or even international collaboration.

The relations between school and government, school and family, school and community are also changing. These relations are productive and rich, and are creating a new ecology of school leadership; the negative concept of *guanxi*, the network of personal influence that principals once relied on to get resources and support, is changing into a positive 'relationship' and leading to more collaboration, more learning and more development.

Sphere pursuit

The traits of leaders are important, but they should not be exaggerated, nor isolated from the context. In Chinese culture, we prefer to relate the leader to leadership, and we asses leaders in a real context (Figure 8.7). Thus we can speak of people acting 'in their sphere' and so assess their quality and state, whether at work or in their daily lives (Fung, 1948).[4]

Through decades of endeavour, Chinese principals have been striving to attain a new state of leadership and to better qualify themselves for the tasks they face.

FIGURE 8.7

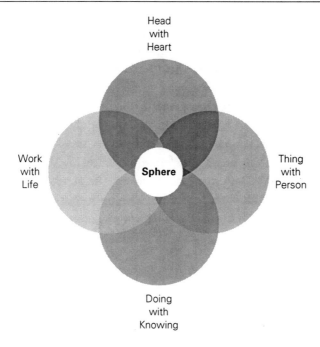

Head and heart

Leadership needs both rationality and passion. Chinese principals have a great tradition: 'doing with heart'. The principal loves the school and sees it as his/her own home; principals care for their colleagues and take the students and teachers as family members; they are eager to do better and devote nearly all their time to it. In this way, school development becomes part of their lives. In Chinese culture, there is a philosophy of life that highlights the belief that the *meaning of life is in the moral, material and rhetorical*. This is still the basis of modern Chinese work and life.

With the development of modern society, Chinese principals are learning more about schooling and leadership, and their understanding is growing through 'doing the right thing' and 'doing things right'. The notions of planning, reflecting and process have been studied, focused and put forward.

The heart and head are integrated in the process of leadership, undivided, supporting and generating each other. Such a leader is a real person: not a machine or fantasy, but one who leads with love, passion, enthusiasm, reflection and complex thinking.

Doing with knowing

Knowledge arises in action and for the action, and we can learn by doing. On the other hand, doing should be based on knowing, and we should communicate our knowledge to one another. In Chinese culture, doing and knowing are not separated; they integrate with each other, and doing often comes first. It is this, we may say, that leads to action-based leadership informed by knowledge and understanding.

In such rapidly changing times, with no model or established precedents, and no tutors, principals have to learn by doing, and to do their tasks with knowledge that is increased and enriched by experience.

We call this *research-based transformative action* (Ye, 2004, 2006). Who are the researchers? The principals! Who are the actors? The principals! They are working with inquiring minds, with both courage and rationality, learning from experience, accumulating knowledge positively and forging the Chinese school leadership.

Work–life balance

A workaholic does not have a rich life, and conversely life cannot be sustained without work. Chinese culture integrates work and life, and respects a person's awareness of living.

In cities, with their busy working rhythms, principals and teachers often worked day and night, even when ill. In rural areas, the quality of schooling and leadership allowed more productive working and a better balance between life and work. This points to the need for a different way of working and living.

A new working style is developing, with a focus on productivity, responsibility and accountability. At the same time, the health of teachers and principals is more highly valued than before, so different kinds of activities are recommended in their spare time. Even more importantly, the leaders' and teachers' families can participate in the life of the school, and the school as a *family* is also based on an ethic of friendship and respect.

Work and personal development

The principal should develop benefits not only for the teachers and students, but also for himself/herself. With the development of the learning-organization and learning-society, the principal must learn to be (International Commission on the Development of Education, 1972).

There are many ways of learning: in universities or academies, through visits organized by local government, or tutoring by experienced principals. Of all the ways, learning and developing in the workplace is the most important. This is expressed in the belief that 'a person develops through achieving things, and a good worker can do more successfully'. In the United States Jim Collins focused on the timeless principles of 'good to great', among them: 'first who... then what' (Collins, 2001). But Chinese principals may disagree with this: for them, the process is integrated. Actually, more development occurs as in-service learning, and principals can be educated better in the field than in the university.

Better working, better development. This cycle makes leadership richer and more rewarding; learning comes through daily life, and leading comes from leaders who are themselves developing.

The new direction

Good to great

Rome was not built in one day, and the sense of '*work in progress*' is clear for Chinese principals.

There are still problems in the collaboration of schools with parents and the community. In 2009, Shanghai took part in the OECD Programme for International Student Assessment (PISA) and achieved the highest score. But if we look at the data on parents' involvement in schools, there is a big gap or big problem compared with other countries (OECD, 2010). Areas where coordination is weak include:

- parents' reluctance to discuss their child's behaviour or progress with a teacher on their own initiative;
- reluctance to discuss their child's behaviour or progress on the initiative of one of the child's teachers;
- lack of volunteers to take part in physical or extra-curricular activities, or to help in the school library or media centre; to assist a teacher in the school; appear as a guest speaker;
- reluctance to participate in the local school government.

Despite these problems, Chinese principals are responsible for running their schools with the support of parents and the community so as to provide great learning and schooling.

Teaching and learning-centred leadership is also a great challenge for principals. Chinese students have a tradition of working hard, but are less proficient at learning in life and with life, or learning through inquiry-based activity and problem solving. Teachers thus face a demanding challenge: to forge a new life style of learning and encourage lifelong development. In some rural areas and in west China, due to weak support from the government, teachers are at a particular disadvantage. Yet, building on a long history and a culture of learning, principals may lead schools into a new era with an active learning culture.

Achieving that comprehensive development is the third great task. In the first part of the 20th century, many of our predecessors worked to establish a new education system; they included leaders such as Yuanpei Cai, Xingzhi Tao, Yanpei Huang, Bolin Zhang and Ziyi Yu. A hundred years later, what will a school in the new century be like? No one knows, but we must try to achieve the goal. A school is a complex system that develops integrally and comprehensively, and the principal is the key to the process.

Practice to theory

Principals work on the basis of research done by many scholars engaged in a range of programmes. Due to the short history of school leadership research and the lack of experience, however, there is still a long way to go.

In developing a Chinese school leadership theory, principals need to cooperate with academic scholars, basing their work on recent innovations in school leadership and putting China's great tradition of education into a modern context. Chinese culture is unique, and Chinese school leadership theory needs be developed differently from that of the West and from the theory of business management.

National to international

In such an interlinked world, communicating and learning internationally is becoming more and more urgent. Collaboration among schools at the national level is becoming easier, but it is still hard to do this internationally.

Chinese principals are focusing on internal development; less attention is paid to international links, and opportunities to visit other countries are limited too, especially for principals in rural areas and west China. While Chinese principals are eager to learn from others, and willing to communicate with their foreign counterparts, the support system is weak. With the globalization of education, however, more and more foreign principals are visiting China, and this will create more opportunities for Chinese principals to share ideas.

At the same time, many international organizations are undertaking research and helping to develop communications between countries. Chinese principals need to be more involved in these activities, attend more international conferences and engage in visits.

In short, Chinese school leadership has its own character, and we need more involvement, more learning and more dialogue.

The author is grateful for funding support from MOE of China and East China Normal University (funding grant 11JJD880013).

Notes

1 The phrase 'big-hand in small-hand' describes a project similar to the 'Big Brother, Big Sister' in America, though it is undertaken in individual schools across different grades. The students engage in a wide range of activities and so help and learn from each other. It is popular in Chinese schools.

2 Chinese schools, unlike their US counterparts, always have a number of teachers for each subject at each grade. In a 'research-class' they will plan a lesson together for a particular class. One will then conduct the lesson, which is always observed by a number of colleagues. and both the teacher and the observers will assess the teaching, and discuss the plan and results, and give feedback to the teacher.

3 In China, the best teachers in a school or district may be designated 'top teachers'. As well as teaching in their own schools, they will coach some other teachers, and the district or school will support them with money and other resources. Thus a new organization will be formed, and the top teachers will lead it, and teach many other teachers. Such an organization is known as a 'lab' because it is used to research and explore new ways of learning.

4 'Sphere' is a Chinese philosophical term that describes a person's attitude of life. The philosopher Yu-Lan Fung (1948) said: 'In my book, *The New Treatise on the Nature of Man*, I have observed that man differs from other animals in that when he docs something, he understands what he is doing, and is conscious that he is doing it. It is this understanding and self-consciousness that give significance for him to what he is doing. The various significances that thus attach to his various acts, in their totality, constitute what I call his sphere of living. Different men may do the same things, but according to their different degrees of understanding and self-consciousness, these things may have varying significance to them. Every individual has his own sphere of living, which is not quite the same as that of any other individual. Yet in spite of these individual differences, we can classify the various spheres of living into four general grades. Beginning with the lowest, they are: the innocent sphere, the utilitarian sphere, the moral sphere, and the transcendent sphere.'

References

Arends, R and Kilcher, A (2010) *Teaching for Student Learning: Becoming an accomplished teacher*, Routledge, New York

Biesta, G (2011) *Learning Democracy in School and Society: Education, lifelong learning and the politics of citizenship*, Sense Publishers, Rotterdam

Bollnow, OF (1999) *Pedagogical Anthropology*, East China Normal University Press, Shanghai

Bolman, L and Deal, T (2011) *Leading with Soul: An uncommon journey of spirit*, revised 3rd edn, Jossey-Bass, San Francisco

Boyer, E (1995) *The Basic School: A community for learning*, The Carnegie Foundation For The Advancement Of Teaching, Princeton, NJ

Bransford, J, Brown, A and Cocking, R (eds) (2000) *How People Learn: Brain, mind, experience, and school* (expanded edition), National Academies Press, Washington, DC

Bronfenbrenner, U (1979) *The Ecology of Human Development: Experiments by nature and design*, Harvard University Press, Cambridge, Mass

Brophy, J, Alleman, J and Knighton, B (2010) *A Learning Community in the Primary Classroom*, Routledge, New York

Collins, J (2001) *Good to Great*, HarperCollins Publishers, New York

Darling-Hammond, L (1994) *Professional Development Schools: Schools for developing a profession*, Teachers College Press, New York

Darling-Hammond, L, Barron, B, Pearson, PD, Schoenfeld, AH, Stage, EK, Zimmerman, TD, Cervetti, GN and Tilson, JL (2008) *Powerful Learning: What we know about teaching for understanding*, Jossey-Bass, San Francisco

Darling-Hammond, L, Meyerson, D, LaPointe, M and Orr, M (2010) *Preparing Principals for a Changing World: Lessons from effective school leadership programs*, Jossey-Bass, San Francisco

Davies, B (ed) (2009) *The Essentials of School Leadership*, 2nd edn, Sage, London

Demarest, E (2010) *A Learning-Centered Framework for Education Reform: What does it mean for national policy?* Teachers College Press, New York

Dewey, J (1916) *Democracy and Education: An Introduction to the philosophy of education*, Macmillan, New York

Dewey, J (1959) *The Child and the Curriculum and The School and Society*, The University of Chicago Press, Chicago

Donovan, MS and Bransford, J (eds) (2005) *How Students Learn: History, mathematics, and science in the classrooms*, National Academies Press, Washington, DC

Dumont, H, Istance, D and Benavides, F (2010) *The Nature of Learning: Using research to inspire practice*, OECD, Paris

Fullan, M (1993) *Change Forces: Probing the depths of educational reform*, Routledge, New York

Fullan, M (1999) *Change Forces: The sequel*, Routledge, New York

Fullan, M (2005) *Leadership and Sustainability: System thinkers in action*, Corwin, Thousand Oaks, Calif

Fung, Y (1948) *A Short History of Chinese Philosophy*, Macmillan, New York

Goodlad, J (1984) *A Place Called School: Prospects for the future*, McGraw-Hill, New York

Guthrie, J and Schuermann, P (2010) *Successful School Leadership: Planning, politics, performance, and power*, Allyn & Bacon, Boston, Mass

Hargreaves, A (2003) *Teaching in the Knowledge Society: Education in the age of insecurity*, Teachers College Press, New York

Hopkins, D (2007) *Every School a Great School: Realizing the potential of system leadership*, Open University Press, Maidenhead

International Commission on the Development of Education (1972) *Learning to Be: The world of education today and tomorrow*, UNESCO, Paris

Jackson, P (1968) *Life in classrooms*, Holt, Reinhart and Winston, New York

Jackson, P (1990) *Life in Classrooms*, new edition, Teachers College Press, New York

Jackson, P (1992) *Untaught Lessons*, Teachers College Press, New York

Jackson, P, Boostrom, R and Hansen, D (1998) *The Moral Life of Schools*, Jossey-Bass, San Francisco

Jarvis, P (2009) *Learning to be a Person in Society*, Routledge, London, New York

Labaree, D (2010) *Someone Has to Fail: The zero-sum game of public schooling*, Harvard University Press, Boston, Mass

Li, Jiacheng (2006a) *Caring for Life: School reform in China*, Educational Science Publishing House, Beijing

Li, Jiacheng (2006b) *Development Needs: In the transition from high school student to college student*, Tianjin Education Press, Tianjin

Li, Jiacheng (2007) Child development and education reform, in L Ye (ed) *Education Philosophy*, People's Education Press, Beijing

Li, Jiacheng (2008) Update of principals' thinking mode in school reform, *Journal of People's Education*, 3–4, pp 22–24

Li, Jiacheng (2010) Values and goals of schooling, in X Yang (ed), *Principals of Education Science*, East China Normal University Press, Shanghai

Li, Jiacheng, Chen, Y and Deng, R (2006) *Reflection on Chinese High School: By post-high school students*, Tianjin Education Press, Tianjin

Li, Jinchu (2006) Develop research-based high schools, *Journal of People's Education*, 17, pp 12–13

Militello, M, Rallis, S and Goldring, E (2009) *Leading With Inquiry and Action: How principals improve teaching and learning*, Corwin, Thousand Oaks, Calif

Morin, E (2004) *Theory of Complexity and Topics of Education*, Peking University Press, Beijing

Murphy, J, Elliott, S, Goldring, E and Porter, A (2006) *Learning-Centered Leadership: A conceptual foundation*, Report Prepared for the Wallace Foundation Grant on Leadership Assessment

Null, J and Ravitch, D (2006) *Forgotten Heroes of American Education: The great tradition of teaching teachers*, Information Age Publishing, Greenwich, Conn

OECD (2010) *PISA 2009 Results: What makes a school success?* (Vol IV), OECD, Paris

Owen, H (2007) *Creating Leaders in the Classroom: How teachers can develop a new generation of leaders*, Routledge, London

Rath, T and Conchie, B (2008) *Strengths Based Leadership*, Gallup Press, New York

Ravitch, D (2010) *The Death and Life of the Great American School System*, Basic Books, New York

Rose, M (2009) *Why School?* The New Press, New York

Sawyer, RK (2006) *The Cambridge Handbook of the Learning Sciences*, Cambridge University Press, New York

Southworth, G (2009) Learning-centred leadership, in B Davies (ed) *The Essentials of School Leadership* (2nd edn), Sage, London

Wagner, T, Kegan, R, Lahey, LL, Lemons, RW, Garnier, J, Helsing, D, Howell, A and Rasmussen, HT (2006) *Change Leadership: A practical guide to transforming our schools*, Jossey-Bass, San Francisco

Wepner, S and Hopkins, D (eds) (2011) *Collaborative Leadership in Action*, Teachers College Press, New York

Willis, JW (2011) Making evaluation useful: improving partnerships through ongoing collaborative assessment, in S Wepner and D Hopkins (eds), *Collaborative Leadership in Action*, Teachers College Press, New York

Wu, H (2009) *On the Relationship of School and University in Collaborative Research*, East China Normal University, Shanghai

Wu, Z and Li, J (2007) *Reform of School Leadership in Chinese School Development*, Educational Science Publishing House, Beijing

Yang, X (2002) *On the Methodology of School Reform in a Changing Time*, East China Normal University Press, Shanghai

Ye, L (1997) Let the classroom be full of vitality, *Educational Research*, 9, pp 3–8

Ye, L (ed) (1999) *Reports on 'New Basic Education' (1994–1999)*, Shanghai Sanlian Publishing House, Shanghai

Ye, L (ed) (2004) *Reports on 'New Basic Education' (1999–2004)*, Chinese Light Industry Press, Beijing

Ye, L (2006) *On 'New Basic Education'*, Educational Science Publishing House, Beijing

Ye, L (ed) (2009) *Reports on 'New Basic Education' (2004–2009)*, Guangxi Normal University Press, Guilin

Ye, L, Li, Z et al (2010) *History of 'New Basic Education' Research*, Educational Science Publishing House, Beijing

Ye, L, Li, Z and Wu, Y (2007) On the transformation of assessment in the school reform, *Journal of Education Development*, 4A, pp 1–10

Leadership in adversity

09

BRIAN PATTERSON

The context for leadership

Ireland is a small country, with a young population. A sovereign state for less than four generations, we are the product of a turbulent history. Our small population is densely interwoven and networked – the six degrees of separation probably shrink to two in Ireland. Irish people are generally friendly, vibrant, expressive, out-going. We don't have a long-standing, established class system and so you would expect Irish people to be less inclined to deference. But centuries of colonial rule have left an ingrained reluctance to 'speak truth to power' – except in a new, younger generation, more self-confident and raised on a daily diet of UK and US media. While there isn't a big right–left divide in politics and social attitudes, trades unions have traditionally been strong – although they are now confined mainly to the public sector.

As a small, island nation, we are open to ideas and influence from many parts of the world. Ireland has close ties with both the United Kingdom and the United States, through centuries of emigration and, more recently, the pervasive influence of both their cultures and media on Ireland. We inherited our legal system and many of our ideas about leadership from Norman England, although these have evolved over the years to an Irish hybrid.

Ireland was late into industrialization. As a result, a large proportion of our people in cities are only first or second generation 'blow-ins'. We carry with us many rural values, including a strong attachment to property, which makes us innately conservative. But because laws were, for centuries, the laws of a foreign power, attitudes to public order and law enforcement are often ambivalent. For example, when approaching a speed trap, many cars driving in the opposite direction will flash their headlights to warn oncoming drivers! Some politicians who have been found guilty of corruption or other bad behaviour continue to get elected. Social responsibility and the concept of civil society are less grounded than in longer-established democracies. When things go wrong, as they have, there is a strong urge to blame 'someone else' and to find scapegoats.

With our membership of the EU, and a young, well-educated, English-speaking population, Ireland has been successful over many years in attracting foreign direct investment. The leadership styles of US and other multinationals have 'trickled out' into Irish organizations. Together with membership of the EU and openness to UK and US media, this has been a modernizing influence in an otherwise traditional society.

Upheavals of the last decade and its effect on leadership

Three recent crises have brought about a major shift in attitudes to leadership.

Boom to bust

In a relatively short time, Ireland has gone from boom to bust. A 10-year debt and property-led bubble brought about a dramatic increase in wealth and living standards. We were 'The Celtic Tiger', the envy of economists and politicians, a poster-child for market-led, lightly regulated, rapid growth. The government of the day was re-elected on a platform of growth and spending. The public coffers were overflowing with property-related taxes, public sector wages raced ahead – and it seemed there was no project too big or too glamorous. The media lionized developers and bankers – none more so than the leaders of Anglo-Irish, a new, brash business bank that blazed a trail of speculative lending and left its competitors gasping for breath. The cult of the heroic leader was everywhere. And they were all men. Government and its cheerleaders poured petrol on the fire, driving the economy faster and faster with tax breaks and more spurs to lending. GDP growth of 8–10 per cent was now accepted as the norm.

Looking back, this was all hubris. The world seemed to contain only easy options, and a generation was brought up on rocketing property prices, conspicuous consumption, celebrity culture, greed and good times. Rights were more important than responsibilities. If some of the excesses were vulgar and there was a coarsening of public life, this was seen as part of Ireland growing up and taking its place amongst the rich countries of the world. Our society enjoyed a decade of partying, with no thought of the hangover that tomorrow would bring.

The bust, when it inevitably came, was dramatic. The credit crunch, the collapse of Lehman Brothers, the international recession, the euro crisis – all hit the overheated Irish economy like a tsunami. The property bubble burst and everything went into reverse. As the tide went out, Ireland was suddenly seen to be 'swimming naked'.

Banks were over-exposed to risk and had borrowed heavily on international markets to fund their growth and rocketing share prices; when the credit crunch came, the banks faced a severe liquidity crisis, which soon became a solvency crisis. As the crisis deepened, under pressure from the European Central Bank (ECB) a major banking crisis was averted at the midnight hour. The government's decision to guarantee all deposits and bonds was a commitment that later would cost the Irish taxpayer dearly. Government revenues depended on a narrow base of property taxes; as the property market froze, tax revenues plummeted and the public finances lurched into deficit. As the euro crisis unfolded, a weakened Ireland was effectively unable to fund its sovereign debt in spooked bond markets – and so had to be bailed out by the 'troika' – the IMF, ECB and EU.

The consequent – and necessary – austerity programme is depressing economic activity still further. Unemployment is rising, emigration has re-started, young couples are in negative equity, unfinished 'ghost' estates blight the landscape and office blocks stand empty. People have seen their savings wiped out, with social welfare benefits and spending on education and health all being cut. Household debt in Ireland is among the highest in the EU. A new depression stalks the land. And there's more austerity to come. Despite the fact the our material standard of living is still far higher than in the mid-1980s – and considerably higher than in most parts of the world – people still feel disadvantaged, let down and cheated. It's someone else's fault. Leaders. Leadership is in the dock – and anyone will do.

Collapse of loyalty to the Church

While the economy was booming, the Catholic Church – which once commanded the loyalty of over 90 per cent of the population and, through centuries of hardship, had been one of the pillars of Irish society – became mired in abuse scandals. Various media and statutory investigations uncovered widespread abuses by a minority of priests and religious orders. This took place in Catholic-run schools, in the Magdalene Laundries (a place of incarceration for women who had been disowned by their families because they became pregnant outside marriage) and in the so-called 'industrial schools' (places of incarceration for orphans and wayward boys) – and in the sacristy itself. This just might have been seen as an embarrassing spotlight on another era and so consigned to history. But it soon became clear that some of the scandals were of more recent vintage. Church leaders, sometimes on advice from lawyers or instructions from Rome, tried to cover up cases of abuse. And they were all men. They failed to recognize and atone for the depth of anger and disappointment that was felt by the victims and loyal believers alike. This culture of denial and failure to face up to its responsibilities resulted in a rapid collapse of the Church's moral authority – particularly among a young, urban and increasingly secular population. Again, leadership was the culprit.

Corruption

There was more. As a result of media and judicial investigations, serious corruption and malpractice were discovered in the body politic – shady links between business and politicians, political leaders on the make, planning scandals. Public servants, once seen as dedicated servants of the nation and the bulwark against political corruption, were in a few cases 'outed' as having been complicit – or in some cases actively involved. Some very costly tribunals of investigation have dragged on for years, feeding the media and the public with a regular stream of new revelations about political corruption and shining a harsh light on a previously hidden world. The idealism of the new republic had given way to dishonesty, fraud and bribery. Hitherto respected leaders were found to have had their 'hands in the till', which destroyed their reputations and brought the whole concept of leadership into disrepute.

A crisis of leadership

So we've had three intertwined crises: the collapse of the banking system and economy, the erosion in support for the church and the discovery of corruption in the body politic. Ireland, once innocently known as 'the island of saints and scholars', is wrestling with a crisis of leadership. Not surprisingly, the media have led a frenzy of blaming and righteous indignation. Scapegoats are easy to find – 'it's all their fault; off with their heads!' A hostile and cynical media has resulted in good people being often afraid to speak up from fear of becoming targets – whether justified or not. As Yeats said, 'The best lack all conviction, while the worst are filled with passionate intensity.'

In the face of these dramatic events, many leaders simply had to go, some admittedly still protesting their innocence. The Fianna Fail government, blamed for wrecking the country, was routed at the last election; banking and business leaders have fallen on their swords – some being investigated for breaches of company law; lawsuits are many; bishops have resigned. A change of government seemed at first to be a breath of fresh air. But, faced with the severe problems they inherited, the new leaders seem to be just more of the same. The public service – and in particular the civil service – seems to continue as if nothing has happened, with an inward-directed, self-perpetuating culture, where 'a safe pair of hands' seems to be valued more than innovation, change and accountability.

The result has been a collapse of old certainties, civilities and loyalties. People feel let down, misled, abandoned. This naturally has fuelled the rise of an angry, if often misinformed, left. There is deep mistrust and cynicism about the institutions of state, business and religion. There is little faith in the future. And at a time when leadership is needed most, leaders – and leadership – are under attack. Followership is in short supply.

A time of opportunity for leaders

But crisis is also a time of opportunity and learning. Irish people are no strangers to adversity and many sensibly and quietly recognize how we got into this mess – and what needs to be done. Blame is slowly turning to acceptance of responsibility – our Taoiseach (Prime Minister) recently said in Davos that we – our society, our institutions – have to accept responsibility for what happened and that greed played a central part in our problems. The howls of protest that this produced were tempered by other voices – a newspaper editorial carried the sarcastic headline 'Nation in shock as politician tells the truth'. The relative austerity now forced on the country is causing a return to more basic and authentic values, as we leave the excesses behind.

Dispersed leadership

People look for leaders who will emerge from the crucible and lead in a new and different way. And as the cult of heroic leadership recedes, we see anew that such leaders are there – and have always been there. We don't see them on our TV screens or in the newspapers, but they are there. They are the living examples, the foot soldiers of dispersed leadership.

These leaders are found on the ground, in organizations large and small, local communities, religious orders. Some examples:

- The MD of a motor distributor, hard hit by the collapse in sales, calls his staff together. Thinking that he is about to announce redundancies, instead they hear him vow to do everything in his power to save their jobs. He leads by taking a pay cut himself and asks for their help in finding imaginative ways of working together that will see their small company through the crisis.

- A priest in a local parish speaks up about the shame he feels at the reports of abuse; he continues to connect with the many who still have faith but have lost their regard for the institutional church.

- A politician stands up to vested interests by going over their heads to the public.

- A bishop speaks the truth about abuse and apologises on behalf of his church.

- A voluntary sector leader includes a compelling video message about the cause the organization serves in its annual report.

- A community leader in a small town mobilizes enterprise to create jobs without any help from the state.

- A journalist swims against the tide to expose the deeper flaws in our society that have led to many of our problems.

- A group of people on both sides of the border work for reconciliation with families and groups from divided communities in Belfast.

Quietly, these are living examples of good, authentic leadership. These are people who:

- are confident in their own abilities and beliefs;

- are accountable to all stakeholders, accepting responsibility;

- practise elements of servant leadership; are in the service of their organizations, their communities, their struggling country; willing to make sacrifices for the greater good, and be the first to pull on the hair shirt;

- are listening and engaged in active, passionate communication;
- are willing to take tough decisions and be held accountable for consequences;
- practise 'good authority' – standing up to vested interests (often in their own ranks) and as necessary being prepared to take on conflict in the service of the majority;
- live clear and good values, consistently and with courage; knowing right from wrong; using their power carefully and wisely;
- have optimism – with a positive mental attitude which transmits itself to others; believing, despite huge difficulties, that we can make things better – that it is 'better to light a candle than to curse the darkness';
- are self-aware – knowing and being comfortable with themselves, their beliefs, their values;
- are in touch with and able to talk about their feelings;
- are open – having the confidence to say 'I don't know', to admit mistakes or weaknesses, to be an 'open book';
- create and articulate a compelling vision, and align and mobilize people behind that vision;
- show humility, respect for and courtesy to others, earning their followership by the strength of their values;
- are resilient – digging deep, to stay the course in tough times; 'holding their shape' in the midst of adversity and cynicism.

The basis of a new leadership

It is from these values that a new leadership will emerge. Because as well as the armies of dispersed leadership, we still also need people who will be at the head – or, as I prefer it, at the centre – of large organizations. These new leaders will shun the cult of the hero. Instead, they will practise their leadership quietly and effectively. They will lead by example and commit their energies to the service of their wider communities. This new style of leadership won't be 'announced'. It's not a programme that can easily be taught in business schools. The situation calls forth a different brand of leadership. It is the quiet and authentic expression of better values that are emerging from the wreckage of recent years. The new leaders will gain confidence and courage by the support they will get from the Irish people.

Power to women

There will also be more women in the ranks of these leaders. Already women are making their presence felt in boardrooms and positions of influence at the centre of organizations. But we need more. The coaching practice of which I am a founder is part of an international effort to increase the number of women in the boardroom through a cross-company mentoring pro-gramme, in which company chairs and chief executives volunteer to mentor a high-potential woman from a different organization (and often a different sector) and to help her break through the glass ceiling. These mentors are chosen for their experience and wisdom. They know that it's not a question of influencing women – consciously or unconsciously – to behave like men. The challenge is to encourage women to express their own gender-based leadership values – values that might have saved us from the worst excesses of the past.

There are at least two excellent Irish role models for women leaders. Ireland has elected two world-class presidents (in the Irish system the presi-dent is the non-political Head of State). Mary Robinson and Mary McAleese served in turn as President from 1990 to 2011; in their different ways, they both brought to the office innovative approaches combined with great dignity. This culminated in the 2011 visit of Queen Elizabeth to Ireland. The visit was heavy with history and symbolism and the quiet dignity of President McAleese and Queen Elizabeth, as they buried centuries of history, captured the hearts of Irish people everywhere.

The power of teams

As we move away from the cult of heroic leadership, leaders are also paying more attention to the latent power that exists in teams. It is no accident that the growth segment of executive coaching is with leadership teams. Like mountaineers, these teams rope themselves together to face into the icy winds and turn their faces to the peaks that must be scaled. Like mountaineers, they relish a challenge and are not put off by setbacks. As the

Irish playwright Samuel Beckett said: 'Ever failed. No matter. Try again. Fail again. Fail better'.

A world without incentives

In parallel with this, there has been a rethink of the role of incentives. Leaders are called to bring about a high performance culture, often without leaning on financial incentives. And they are discovering that it can be done! Sometimes this is by focus on a 'noble cause': one newly appointed CEO of a major public utility took on his demanding role at half the salary of his predecessor and with no bonus entitlement. He did so because he isn't motivated by money, and simply wanted to help his country and its people to recover. He went further and rejoiced in the fact that he was being paid a lot less as this would give him the moral authority to lead his organization through a major restructure and a shift away from a culture of entitlement. Other leaders paint a compelling vision of the future and how we will emerge from all this adversity into a better place – with more sustainable growth and better values.

This evidence on the ground supports some recent psychological experiments about the negative effect of financial incentives – see *Business Week*, 'The dark side of incentives' (12 November 2009), and Daniel Pink on 'The surprising science of motivation' (on **www.ted.com**). These experiments point to the fact that under financial incentives a sense of social responsibility goes out of the window – and also that in all but rudimentary tasks, performance actually suffers.

Rediscovering our strengths

Despite the cataclysms of recent years, Ireland still has a lot of positives. These give us a base on which we can build a better world with a better leadership to shape that world. They include:

- A competitive export sector delivering strong growth – exports were up 5 per cent in 2011, driven by the indigenous agri-food industry and the multi-national sector in pharmaceuticals and information technology. Intel, Google, Adobe, Facebook – and many others – all have major footprints in Ireland.
- A vibrant culture of innovation and business start-ups.

- World-beating state agencies that support inward investment (the Industrial Development Authority) and indigenous development (Enterprise Ireland and Science Foundation Ireland).
- Universities that produce increasing numbers of high-quality, English-speaking graduates.
- Vastly improved infrastructure – transport, schools, telecoms.
- A now more competitive and solid tourism industry.
- Support from our worldwide diaspora (a group of powerful Irish-American CEOs have volunteered their services to the state).
- Punching above our weight in sport and the arts.

Despite all of the problems, Ireland is still ranked the 10th wealthiest country in the OECD.

Northern Ireland

Then, of course, there is the North. This deep-rooted problem has sometimes been described as the problem of two minorities:

- In Northern Ireland the Catholic/Republican population see themselves as an oppressed minority.
- On the whole island, the Protestant/Loyalist population see themselves as a threatened minority.

This Gordian knot led to decades of violence that shamed decent Irish people everywhere. When the divided communities had reached a stage of exhaustion, patient and courageous leaders – and there were very many and at all levels – were able to bring about a fragile peace on which to build. This included mobilizing the people of the Republic to vote, in a referendum, to give up their idealized claim to the territory of Northern Ireland and instead to affirm the right of the people there to decide, by peaceful means, their own future. There is still much work to be done in recognizing deep hurts, reconciling divided communities and reducing sectarianism. But at least the conditions for real progress are now present.

Leaders working for recovery

Back in the South, despite the low level of esteem for politicians generally, our new political leaders have embarked on the tough road of recovery.

Despite the many difficulties face by the 'squeezed middle', people have been willing to follow and to give them support. And while some other countries seem in denial and convulsed with division and conflict, those in Europe and further afield recognize the determination and discipline there is in Ireland to tackle our problems. National self-belief, pride and confidence are slowly returning; financial markets are now requiring a much lower premium on our sovereign debt.

Since the foundation of the Irish State in the 1920s, it has required committed, innovative, courageous and visionary leadership to move us from a poor, agrarian, inward-looking country to a modern industrialized state with internationally traded goods and services and a vibrant role in the EU and the world. The challenge now is to go back to the basics that motivated this transformation and to manage down our debt – while building a more sustainable future. While our current reliance on the troika of the IMF, ECB and EU places limits on our financial independence, we are a small and still independent country. Smallness means we can be agile and nimble on our international feet. Independence means we have our destiny in our own hands. If we mess up again, we have nobody to blame but ourselves. But we also have the freedom to make our own decisions, the freedom to build a new and better country.

More widely, the EU is itself in the throes of intense turmoil and debate about its future shape and destiny. Some would say it is awaiting the emergence of a new leadership, capable of reinvigorating the vision of its founding leaders after the cataclysms of two world wars. With its recent learning and newly emerging leadership, Ireland can perhaps play a creative part in shaping this EU of tomorrow.

A time for optimism

In the midst of adversity, it's easy to follow the line of the naysayers and a lot of our media into blame, cynicism and pessimism. But, as Harvard Professor David Landes says:

> In this world the optimists have it, not because they are always right, but because they are positive. Even when wrong they are positive, and that is the way of achievement, correction, improvement and success. Educated, eyes-open optimism pays; pessimism can only offer the empty consolation of being right. The one lesson that emerges is the need to keep trying. No miracles. No perfection. No millennium. No apocalypse. We must cultivate a sceptical faith, avoid dogma, listen and watch well, try to clarify and define ends, the better to choose means.

So, as we face the future, I am optimistic. We've been in much tougher places than this, and have emerged better and stronger. And a new leadership is emerging that is appropriate to the times and that will serve us better.

The contract

A word from the led

And in the end we follow them –
not because we are paid,
not because we might see some advantage,
not because of the things they have accomplished,
not even because of the dreams they dream,
but simply because of who they are:
the man, the woman, the leader, the boss,
standing up there when the wave hits the rock,
passing out faith and confidence like life-jackets,
knowing the currents, holding the doubts,
imagining the delights and terrors of every landfall;
captain, pirate and parent by turns,
the bearer of our countless hopes and expectations.
We give them our trust. We give them our effort.
What we ask in return is that they stay true.

William Ayot: 'Small Things that Matter'

Leadership
A global reality

10

HILARIE OWEN

The concept of leadership has been written about for at least five thousand years. It is written in hieroglyphic form in the Cairo Museum and there is divided into three words: *Seshemu* (leader), *Seshemet* (leadership) and *Shemsu* (follower). Unlike management, leadership is an ancient concept and one that is used in everyday language. In addition, the language we use is not just a means of communication; it involves thinking and reasoning.

In ancient Chinese writings we learn that if a leader is good it is more likely that those who follow will also be good. If the leader is selfish, so will the followers be selfish. Confucius regarded education as a transformational process that takes place within an individual but does so through conversation with others. Learning through others has been a common theme in the chapters written here from different parts of the world. In other words, learning leadership is not so much an isolated journey as one that exists in a set of relations with others.

Finding what leadership potential you have is not something you do in isolation or on a training course. While the 20th century provided a huge richness of writings on leadership, leadership development in organizations focused on the individual as leader and this has created a gap between theory and practice. As John Gardner wrote: 'We have barely scratched the surface in our effort towards leadership development. In the mid 21st century, people will look back on our present practices as primitive' (Gardner, 1995). Yet, within the mass of writings there were some jewels.

One of the most profound writings of the 20th century on leadership came from Mary Parker Follett, who in a series of papers written for business education during the late 1930s set views of leadership that were to influence others. She began by criticizing two psychologists who viewed leadership as aggressiveness and dominating, a view still held by some today.

Follett believed leadership could come from anywhere, regardless of position. She believed that leadership was about grasping the total situation and the ability to organize everyone to serve a common purpose. This, she said, meant that instead of personal power there was 'group power'.

In addition, Follett said that leadership required a pioneering spirit that would challenge and blaze new trails by seeing possible new paths. In other words leadership took us to new places because it required courage. Her contribution to our understanding of leadership included her ideas about followers, who she believed were not passive but actively helping the leader to stay in control of a situation.

In a lecture she gave in the 1930s she said: 'Let us not think that we are either leaders – or nothing of much importance... Leaders and followers are both following the invisible leader – the common purpose' (quoted in Graham, 1995).

In this way *the success of the team made possible the success of the leader, not the other way around*. Leadership is a dynamic connection between leader and follower. The time for Follett's ideas has arrived, as the chapters here show a shift away from the leader of position or 'hero' to leadership from everywhere in collaboration with others. However, a story by Anthony de Mello (1990) shows the challenge we face:

> A man found an eagle's egg and put it in a nest of a barnyard hen. The eagle hatched with the brood of chicks and grew up with them.
>
> All his life the eagle did what the barnyard chicks did, thinking he was a barnyard chicken. He scratched the earth for worms and insects. He clucked and cackled. And he would thrash his wings and fly a few feet into the air.
>
> Years passed and the eagle grew very old. One day he saw a magnificent bird in the cloudless sky. It glided in graceful majesty among the powerful wind currents, with scarcely a beat of its strong golden wings.
>
> The eagle looked up in awe. 'Who is that?' he asked
>
> 'That's the eagle, the king of the birds,' said his neighbour. 'He belongs to the sky. We belong to the earth – we're chickens.' So the eagle lived and died a chicken, for that's what he thought he was.

In my research with young people, by age 11 only 46 per cent of boys thought they had leadership potential and a staggering low number, 18 per cent, of girls thought they had leadership potential. The main reason was that they didn't think they were good enough. What are we doing to young people in the UK and how are we failing them? Today almost one in five of the people aged between 16 and 24 in the UK are not in education, training or work. They feel there is no future for them and their lives are over before they have even begun. Those who are lucky to go to university are saddled with high fees. We now hear of medical students going into prostitution to pay for their education. So many young people do not value themselves.

We are losing a generation of young people who are needed to shape the future, while we sit back and hope governments will resolve the issue. The problem is one for *all* of us to resolve. We see challenges such as this and feel angry, frustrated and anxious; yet we do nothing. If we shun responsibility, close our doors to the rest of our communities, allow a few leaders to take away what we value – then we have only ourselves to blame. Have we focused so much on the *rights* of the individual that we have lost *responsibility* and *values* in the UK? Why has this happened?

In my work with schools in the UK, teachers said the main barrier to developing leadership in young people was lack of self-confidence and self-belief. For some teachers, this was an issue for them also. Pupils also told us that the biggest barrier to developing leadership in themselves and their peers was lack of confidence and belief in their abilities. In addition, parents told us that they did not want their children to have the low confidence, low self-esteem and low self-belief they had experienced themselves. It became clear that the lack of leadership stemmed from generations, and it was not just our present young people who lacked the confidence to act. Yet as human beings we each have huge potential to use leadership in many positive ways. How do we change this so everyone can express their potential in a world that sorely needs it?

John Gardner (1995) wisely advised: 'The first step is not action; the first step is understanding.'

The first national leadership audit in the UK carried out in 2010 with 1,040 working people to establish how ordinary people felt about leadership in the country today. Some of the highlights of the research were:

- Over 80 per cent of respondents said they did not believe the present leaders could resolve the issues/challenges we face today in the UK.

- 75 per cent said they believed we have a leadership crisis in the UK today.

- Nearly 90 per cent believed there was a leadership crisis in the world.

- Nearly 80 per cent of respondents said they believed that unless leadership improved in the UK we would decline as a nation.

- Over 90 per cent said they believed leaders were out of touch with the average person.

- Almost 100 per cent of respondents said that more should be done to develop leadership in schools, communities and work organizations.

- While over 85 per cent believed they had leadership talent, fewer than half the respondents had ever attended any form of leadership development.

This shows a remarkable need for action, even though millions are spent each year on leadership development. Are the wrong people delivering this? Do they really understand leadership? Are the right people developing their leadership? Are leaders too busy gaining power to realize the impact they are having on others, and do they care?

When the above sample were asked how much confidence they had in the leadership of different people, the military came top, followed by leaders in medicine, with the press, religious leaders and government at the bottom. In the middle were leaders from charities, education, the police and business. Lower down were civil servants, local and national government and religious leaders. This changed when people were asked how much confidence they had in the honesty, integrity and ethics in the professional and personal lives of leaders. For this, leaders of charities and NGOs came top, followed by educational leaders, the police, medicine and military. Business leaders were relegated lower down along with governments and the press.

The straightforward question of who people considered to be the best leaders in the UK today produced the following ranking:

- 68 per cent military;
- 66 per cent family members;
- 64 per cent NHS surgeons;
- 61 per cent university professors;
- 60 per cent chief constables;
- 59 per cent head teachers;
- 56 per cent charity CEOs;
- 54 per cent business leaders;
- 53 per cent the Queen;
- 49 per cent senior civil servants;
- 46 per cent the prime minister (regardless of party);
- 46 per cent church leaders;
- 35 per cent newspapers and TV editors.

It should be noted that this study took place shortly before the 'phone hacking' scandal had become so notorious. The 1,040 people surveyed were all of working age, with the majority in their thirties and forties. Talking to retired people might have resulted in a slightly different response, but these are the parents and future parents of people in the UK. When asked what they believed were the greatest leadership challenges for us today the following was found:

- 89 per cent the economy;
- 81 per cent crime;
- 79 per cent immigration;
- 77 per cent the environment;
- 76 per cent terrorism;
- 75 per cent education;
- 73 per cent health;
- 72 per cent depreciation of values in society;
- 72 per cent religious hatred;
- 71.5 per cent wars;
- 70 per cent poverty;
- 67.5 per cent breakdown of families;
- 65 per cent loss of community life;
- 64 per cent work–life balance;
- 64 per cent the elderly;
- 62.5 per cent corruption;
- 60.5 per cent too much emphasis on profits;
- 59.5 per cent over-consumerism;
- 49 per cent obsession with celebrity.

Finally, people were very clear about what they expected from good leadership. The question 'How important are each of the following criteria to good leadership?' produced the following responses, ranked in order with the top three far outweighing the rest on the list. Leaders should learn from this.

- 92 per cent ability to communicate;
- 91 per cent honesty and integrity;
- 91 per cent trust;
- 86 per cent decisiveness;
- 83 per cent taking charge;

- 82 per cent open mindedness;
- 80 per cent empathy with others;
- 79.6 per cent cooperating with others;
- 71 per cent charisma;
- 70 per cent challenging the status quo.

People in the UK believe there is a leadership crisis and that we are not addressing this crisis for the present needs and future generations. It's not that organizations and governments are not doing anything to address this – they are, but they do not seem to be doing the right things. It has been estimated that at least £120million was spent on leadership development in the UK in 2010. The fact is that developing leadership is very different from developing management skills or IT skills and it is this issue – how young people and adults learn leadership – that has been the focus of my work with colleagues in other parts of the world as well as the UK.

The challenge, as the above research clearly shows, is about developing far more leadership capability across society because unless we do the world will never address the real challenges it faces.

It is as John Gardner (1995) concludes:

> Most men and women go through their lives using no more than a fraction – usually a rather small fraction – of the potentialities within them. The reservoir of unused human talent and energy is vast, and learning to tap that reservoir more effectively is one of the exciting tasks ahead for humankind.
>
> Among the untapped capabilities are leadership gifts. For every effectively functioning leader in our society, I would guess there are five or ten others with the same potential for leadership who have never led or perhaps even considered leading. Why? Perhaps they were drawn off by the byways of specialization... or have never sensed the potentialities within them... or have never understood how much the society needs what they have to give.
>
> We can do better. Much, much better.

How can we do better? Each of the leadership educators in this book is contributing every day, in positive ways, to enable leadership potential to grow. Through this understanding, barriers that need to be overcome are becoming clear. We have focused on what makes a leader but we also need to explore what prevents leadership. To change people's paradigms, mindsets, mental models, thinking and beliefs is the next huge step. Before there is behavioural change there needs to be cognitive change. We live our lives on the basis of our beliefs, assumptions and expectations every day. Physicist and philosopher David Bohm (1996) wrote: 'To think differently – this thought must enter deeply into our intentions, actions and so on – our whole being.'

There are two steps to doing this. The first is to feel dissonance with the old paradigm; the second is to not just understand but also connect with the new paradigm, mental model etc, and a way of doing this is through dialogue. The rest of this chapter will clarify the two steps and show how great the challenge is – but not impossible.

A new way of seeing the world and ourselves

Thomas Kuhn (1962) coined the term 'paradigm' as a 'constellation of concepts, values, techniques and so on, shared by a (scientific) community'. Fritjof Capra (1997) expanded Kuhn's definition to one that we shall use here: 'a constellation of concepts, values, perceptions and practices shared by a community which forms a particular vision of reality that is the basis of the way the community organizes itself'. That vision of reality includes the belief that only a few can be leaders and that they have positional authority to do so. The majority of young people believe they are not good enough to lead, and that has to change. Our education system is based on the old paradigm and is holding us back. What is that old paradigm?

In the 20th century reality to most people was based on a paradigm known as the 'scientific' or Cartesian paradigm based on Newtonian physics. Things were broken down into parts to be studied in a mechanistic way. Education and medicine still use this. The paradigm enabled the Industrial Revolution and the machines to rule and we learned much about our world. Life was seen as a competitive struggle where individuals felt isolated and apart from nature. It created a world hell-bent on unlimited material progress through economic expansion, requiring more and more to be made and bought. Our education system broke up learning also into separate subjects where you were tested. The outcomes of these tests would influence your role in work and society. They also influenced your income and health.

Out of this Industrial Age paradigm came management that replaced leadership. Management is based on order and control – thriving in hierarchical structures and stability, overseeing a less educated workforce. The rise of the professional manager grew with the MBA and business schools and the belief that managers knew more. For the last 60 years there has been a drive to 'capture' leadership, put it in a box and teach it. In vain, the Western world searched for the 'hero' leader to 'fix' things. No wonder most people projected themselves as 'not a leader' as they regarded themselves as too 'ordinary'. The 'hero' human beings had human frailties too, and sometimes a short 'lifespan' either voluntarily or involuntarily. This is the paradigm that is fixed in the minds of people. Yet it is 'ordinary' people who have expressed leadership when needed. Mrs Parks on the bus refusing to give up her seat to a white man, who encouraged more to campaign against racial discrimination. The three women who set up the Snowdrop campaign after the shooting of children and a teacher in Scotland, who successfully campaigned to ban hand-guns in the UK except in shooting clubs. This is leadership in practice, and it fits with the new paradigm and understanding of the world.

It was Einstein who, having associated the gravitational field with the geometry of space, then brought quantum theory and relativity together to describe the force fields of subatomic particles. He showed that material objects are not separate but linked to their environment and that their properties can only be understood in terms of their interaction with the rest of the world. This interrelationship is crucial to our understanding of the world in the 21st century. Not as a political 'gimmick' or statement but a reality that is about community and leadership.

In quantum theory you do not have things, but interconnections. Particles come into being and are observed only in relationship to something else. One of the pioneers in quantum physics was Werner Heisenberg, who remarked (1971): 'The world thus appears as a complicated tissue of events, in which connections of different kinds alternate or overlap or combine and thereby determine the texture of the whole.'

Here nature consists not of isolated building blocks (or silos) but rather a complex web of relationships between the various parts of a unified whole. Our world isn't a machine-like entity, determined and fixed, but is one of interconnections and interrelationships. Yet we build organizations in fixed structures controlled by 'managers'. Even when we restructure, the fixed pattern of structures and processes remain. We are still seeing organizations in the old paradigm. A huge shift is required in our understanding of the world and how we as humans relate to it and express our leadership. But to do this we have to know our world.

When Einstein wrote his autobiography (1991) he said:

A human is part of the whole, called by us, Universe... He experiences himself, his thoughts and feelings, as something separated from the rest – a kind of optical delusion of his consciousness. This delusion is a kind of prison, restricting us to our personal desires and to affection for a few persons nearest to us. Our task must be to free ourselves from this prison by widening our circle of compassion to embrace all.

Why is it so hard to make the shift? There are two explanations and a clue to how the change can occur to enable more leadership. The first time I tried to understand this problem, it took me to the work of Richard Dawkins who introduces the concept of 'memes' in his book *The Selfish Gene* (1976). He explains that just as genes transport characteristics from one body in a family to another, memes transport human culture from one body to another. Dawkins says: 'Just as genes propagate themselves in the gene pool by leaping from body to body via sperms or eggs, so memes propagate themselves in the meme pool by leaping from brain to brain via a process which, in the broad sense, can be called *imitation*.' This is done through ideas, articles, songs, fashion, ways of making things, doing things and seeing the world.

Dawkins argues that memes are instructions for carrying out behaviours, stored in brains and passed on by imitation. An example of this today in the UK is how young people add the word 'like' to almost every sentence when it is not needed. It may also explain, when researching with young people in schools, why those who suffered from low self-esteem, had a parent with low self-esteem and often a grandparent with low self-esteem.

Memes come to us from parents, teachers, friends, bosses, colleagues, books, films, television, newspapers and so on. Taken together, they become our culture and we believe that how we do things is how everyone else should do things. When we invade another culture, we believe our way is right and that others should copy us. Civilizations have acted on this time and time again, no more so than the British Empire and the United States today.

Dawkins (1976) writes: 'The computers in which memes live are human brains... If a meme is to dominate the attention of the human brain, it must do so at the expense of other rival memes.' Therefore, in order for humans to believe in one god, other gods had to disappear. Yet memes are not easy to dismantle, which is why the Newtonian, mechanistic world is still real to people. Memes like to connect with other memes that complement them, and from this become powerful. An example could the way Margaret Thatcher, as a chemist and lawyer, saw the world through this narrow spectrum of breaking things up, resulting in her statement: 'There's no such thing as society.'

Millions of memes are competing for space in our brains. Those that become strong form into a meme-complex. These are groups of memes that come together for mutual advantage and become a self-organizing, self-protecting structure that welcomes compatible memes and repels others.

In addition, when memes become part of a person's self-concept, they become connected to who that person believes him- or herself to be. To show the power of these replicators, see how people react when change threatens their possessions such as a car-parking space, size and make of car or bonuses. At a Chartered Institute of Management conference I explained how leadership could come from anywhere, only to be met with an angry response of 'Only managers can be leaders!' This was status and self-identity being threatened and a strong meme-complex that made managers feel they were under attack. Even more interesting were the comments at the coffee break, with many saying: 'I can't get my head round what you were saying. It makes my head hurt.'

For me to change my memes means changing myself. In other words, my identity with 'I'm not really a leader' to 'I'm a leader and enjoy leading.' Dawkins believes we can rebel against our memes but it's not easy. He didn't say how we should do this but this is what I have found works:

- There must be the ability to change: for example, to address a fixed mindset (Dweck) and the potential for leadership.
- There needs to be a sense of dissonance or lack of consistency with the old meme: for example, 'I don't feel like a leader but I'm doing leadership things at work.'
- There must be a recognition of what is causing this dissonance.
- One must be aware of an alternative view in order to form a new meme.
- One must identify what barriers are preventing the shift and address each one.
- Realization that change feels difficult and to persevere, even when it feels that it would be easier to return to the 'old' way. The difficulty is due to the way the brain works. It would appear that the brain has a large part to play in changing or developing leadership.
  Understanding this will explain why the managers at the conference remarked that what I was saying made their heads hurt.

The brain and change

As human beings we are bombarded with data every day. The brain copes with it all by being programmed to process information as efficiently as possible with minimum thought and attention. However, the side effect of this is that making change in thinking and behaviour is difficult. Most of the time behaviour, including thinking, is on automatic pilot. Like a software program, the brain takes incoming data, processes it, and classifies the data into existing categories.

As human beings we are neurally programmed to operate mostly from our assumptions and expectations. This automatic brain processing, in the basal ganglia, requires little energy and operates mainly subconsciously.

When faced with a new experience or data that can't be easily classified, our working memory, the prefrontal cortex, tries to match it against previous experiences and give it meaning. If the working memory is involved in new or complex information, that feels like hard work because this part of the brain has limited capacity, is energy intensive and requires focused attention and concentration. We feel hungry or tired and may even say 'my head hurts' to think so hard. This is because we are forging new neural circuits and are literally changing our brain structures and processes.

To change, we must focus our attention for a sustained period of time to make these brain changes. Therefore, for people to change their leadership behaviour, they have to focus on the new behaviour for a specific time, to develop the new neurons. After that, they need opportunities to keep practising so the new neuron becomes strong. The more the new neuron is used, the thicker it actually becomes and the previous connection is eventually replaced. We need to understand this when developing leadership.

Could this be why Warren Bennis and Bob Thomas identified the significance of 'crucible hardships' in the process of learning and developing leadership? However, while Warren and Bob say experience is the key to developing leadership, they clarify this by showing that experience itself is not the nugget but what an individual does with that experience, and the gold nugget is learning. They say: 'what sets these leaders apart is their approach to learning' (Thomas, 2008). What they found was that the best leaders learn while they are doing their work, and in particular when facing new and difficult challenges. In other words, they are using the prefrontal cortex, or working memory, and forming new neural pathways. Thomas writes: 'the ability to learn – and to learn quickly – is an essential part of successful adaptation to the challenges of living in human society, especially in the 21st century' (Thomas, 2008). What is clear is that the brain and learning are fundamental to unlearning and learning leadership. This is totally different from developing management skills, and those that put management and leadership together do so because they do not understand the difference or do not understand how we learn leadership.

Finally, people learn best and most sustainably when, for example, they practise leading and solving problems themselves instead of being told how to by a boss. When this happens, the brain releases a rush of neurotransmitters such as adrenalin. Maintaining that focus to the new insight, the learning then becomes part of the new structure of the brain. Contrast this with flashes of insights from training programmes that never translate into new thinking or behaviour changes.

What hinders our learning is when anxiety or fear is triggered in the amygdala, or the emotional brain. It drains neural energy from the pre-frontal region and can result in defensive behaviour that blocks learning. Bennis and Thomas found that the best leaders don't become paralysed or stuck. Chaos doesn't throw them because they see these challenges as opportunities to learn and grow. While in a difficult situation they are resilient, communicate constantly with honesty that engages people to go with them, and when it's over both the leader and organization have transformed. This sets the tone for others to become learning leaders.

To go beyond leaders to leadership throughout the organization, a better option than training is a series of master classes with space in between for dialogue. This can be supplemented with mentoring. The most important element is the space in between for dialogue and reflective learning.

Dialogue to move forward

The roots of dialogue are with the Greek philosopher Socrates. In 1914, the philosopher Martin Buber used the term to mean more than a discussion, and instead said it was a way for people to appreciate each other as human beings. However, it is the work of physicist David Bohm that has contributed most to the concept of dialogue that has now been taken up by William Isaacs at MIT in the United States.

Bohm suggested that dialogue should be a form of conversation that focuses on bringing to the surface and altering the 'tacit infrastructure' of thought. He believed that when groups of individuals learned to watch and articulate, the assumptions inherent in both individual and collective thought may alter their self-defeating and self-deceptive processes. In other words, through dialogue the brain is focusing on the pre-frontal cortex (thinking brain) and not allowing the amygdala (emotional brain) to interfere. Thus it can produce new neural connections for new ways of thinking and meaning. When people talk, they share not only words but meaning.

An example of this is from a conversation I had with the lovely British MP Mo Mowlam about her experience of the peace process in Northern Ireland, where she served as Secretary of State. She told me how she encouraged different sides to talk about how they perceived things in different rooms (they wouldn't sit in the same room at this stage). The assumptions, beliefs and fears all came out. But it was the Women's Coalition that also made an important step as they were the only ones who would stand up to the Reverend Ian Paisley, who would blast his anger on anyone who disagreed with him. Over time, conversations became easier as a result of deep dialogue and the thinking brain being able to focus – not always, but enough to override the emotional brain.

What is the present behaviour of those in your organization? What are the leadership behaviours that are required?

It is through collective dialogue that movement begins. Dialogue explores our closely held values, the nature and intensity of our emotions, the patterns of our thought processes, our mental models, our memory, inherited cultural myths and beliefs, the way we structure moment-to-moment experience and the way thought is generated at a collective level. The process questions our deeply held assumptions, beliefs, culture, meaning and identity – in other words, our paradigms. It even tests our definitions of work, organizations and life.

Learning leadership requires us to question our assumptions and self-defeating thinking. From this new insight we can see what is possible, and with it the changes in behaviour that are required. Through dialogue with others and through different experiences, individuals learn to suspend their defensive exchanges and ask why those exchanges exist. It often means struggling to understand (using the working brain rather then the automatic brain), building a confidence in a new tomorrow after the scepticism drawn from the past, and coming to terms with the realization that leadership can come from anywhere. But it's hard work and control will need to be replaced with trust.

Dialogue should continue until there is change, though over-persuasion is not called for. The process isn't easy and can be frustrating at times as individuals become aware of their own reactions and feelings: 'I don't know how to resolve this,' 'No one has expected me to do this before,' 'I'm frightened of making a mistake.' At these times, it is tempting to step in, but the learning should come from within people rather than the outside world.

When change occurs collectively, it is very powerful and the opportunity arises to work with others making the transition to the new. Everyone should be involved in this, including those at the top of the present hierarchy. For the future is created by all the people with aspirations, values and growing expectations that they are responsible for. As psychologist Alberto Bandura wrote: 'Human lives are highly interdependent. What they do individually affects the well-being of others, and in turn, what others do affects their personal well-being. People must increasingly work together to make a better life for themselves' (Bandura, 1997).

There is a saying: you never change things by fighting the existing reality. To change something, build a new model that makes the existing model obsolete. What is happening here is the building of a new meme-complex.

As human beings we have two things that make us unique while connected to the rest of life: our brains and our language. In learning and advancing leadership in the world today, we need to utilize both. It is through leading with others that is the future. The evidence is here in this book. Then we *can* do better. But it begins with each one of us finding our own leadership and putting it into practice every day. As Warren Bennis (1989) says: 'By the time we reach puberty, the world has reached us and shaped us to a greater extent than we realize. Our family, friends, school and society in general have told us – by word and example – how to be. But people begin to become leaders at that moment when they decide for themselves how to be.'

I have seen this happen when my son, an athlete, worked with young teenagers who had been excluded from schools. Through sport he helped them develop self-esteem and belief in themselves and that life didn't have to be as it was for their parents. As they focused their thinking and beliefs, their anger and self-loathing was replaced with self-respect and knowing how to change their lives for the better. Around the world people are engaging to change things. When ordinary people do extraordinary things the world does change for the better... It's called leadership.

References

Bandura, A (1997) *Self Efficacy: The exercise of control*, WH Freeman, New York
Bennis, W (1989) *On Becoming a Leader*, Addison Wesley, Reading, Mass
Bohm, D (1996) *In Dialogue*, Routledge, London
Capra, F (1997) *The Web of Life*, Harper Collins, New York
Dawkins, R (1976) *The Selfish Gene*, Oxford University Press, Oxford
De Mello, A (1990) Song of the bird, in A De Mello, *Awareness*, Harper Collins, London

Einstein, A (1991) Autobiographical notes, in *The World Treasury of Physics, Astronomy and Mathematics*, ed Timothy Ferris, pp 577–90, Little Brown & Co, New York

Gardner, JW (1995) The cry for leadership, in *The Leader's Companion*, ed J Thomas Wren, pp 3–7, Simon & Schuster, New York

Graham, P (ed) (1995) *Prophet of Management: Mary Parker Follett*, Harvard Business School Press, Cambridge, Mass

Heisenberg, W (1971) *Physics and Beyond*, Harper Collins, New York

Kuhn, T (1962) *The Structure of Scientific Revolutions*, University of Chicago Press, Chicago

Owen, H (2010) UK Leadership Audit Report, Institute of Leadership

Ross C (2011) *The Leaderless Revolution*, Simon & Schuster, New York

Thomas R (2008) *Crucibles of Leadership*, Harvard Business Press, Boston, Mass

INDEX

(*italics* indicates a figure in the text)

CPSIA information can be obtained at www.ICGtesting.com
Printed in the USA
LVOW070814060213

PP7373100001B/1/P